ANITA'S WAR

ANITA'S WAR

From Stalin and Hitler to Freedom in Christ

REBECCA MORRIS BARBER

Dallas, Texas
ICR.org

ANITA'S WAR
From Stalin and Hitler to Freedom in Christ

by Rebecca Morris Barber

First printing: September 2023

Unless otherwise specified, all Scripture quotations are from the King James Version.

ISBN: 978-1-946246-93-6
Library of Congress Catalog Number: 2023945768

Please visit our website for other books and resources: ICR.org

Printed in the United States of America.

Published by Wayfinders Press, an imprint of ICR Publishing Group

Table of Contents

Anita's Family

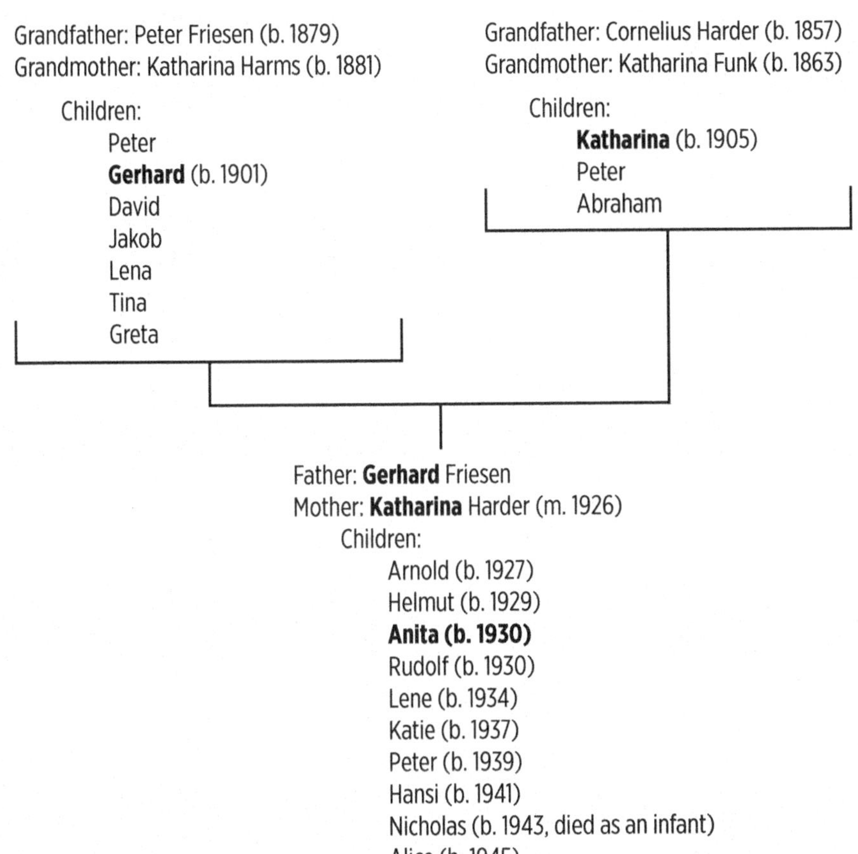

Foreword

The person you will read about in the pages that follow came from the darkest of situations into God's marvelous light. Heroes come from varied backgrounds and places. They often arise out of the most difficult circumstances.

Anita Friesen was born into a decidedly Christian family of Mennonite heritage between the World Wars, but her parents were forbidden from passing this knowledge on to her. Living in Germany, Mennonite farming families like the Friesens eventually migrated to Ukraine to escape persecution. But soon godless communism captured Ukraine. A sharp student willing to please her teachers, Anita learned to recite the communist pledge and revere Stalin. She knew nothing of her parents' love for God and the Bible. Such knowledge was forbidden.

As World War II spread, the Russian motherland forced Anita's entire farming village to abandon their homes and begin traveling eastward, a journey that was interrupted when the Nazis captured control of Ukrainian territory. Her Mennonite community and family returned to their homes where the church was reopened and the Bible gladly brought out of hiding. But Anita had learned not to listen to such things. Under German occupation, students in school learned different creeds once again and how to salute Hitler. She joined the Hitler Youth and supported Nazism.

As the war faded to a close, the Soviets began retaking Ukrainian territory, and Anita's village was again forced to evacuate. This second journey was halted when the war ended. But what was next? There was no place they could call home. Germany no longer wanted them, and a return to the USSR meant a labor camp in Siberia.

A door opened for them to immigrate to the jungles of South America where Anita eventually obtained a nursing career and married an American soldier. In God's sovereignty, her husband learned of the gospel, and God used this and other circumstances to draw Anita to Himself. She finally opened her heart to Jesus, and the years that followed saw her victoriously launch a fruitful life and Christian ministry.

Anita grew up as a child and young adult under oppressive regimes that stifled freedom and exercised complete control over their citizens. She was indoctrinated with man-centered and God-eschewing beliefs, enduring extreme hardships and dangers. But God brought Anita through it and led her to a saving knowledge of His Son. With the example of her journey, maybe we and our children can recognize the darkness present around us today and choose God's light.

Dr. John Morris
ICR President Emeritus

Introduction

"You just don't know how good you have it." How often do children of every generation hear these words growing up? My parents lived through difficult times. Yet I look at children growing up today, and I suspect their lives are just as hard but in an entirely different way. Video games, TV commercials, and never-ending messages from the internet dominate their minds. These sound bites drown out the quiet voices of self-reflection, reason, and conscience. There's precious little blank space to think. That's why it's easier to simply believe what you are told to believe.

Idolatrous worldviews are rampant in today's society. They can be found in public education and mainstream science. Believing that humans are simply another class of animal, selected by blind nature—the result of a cosmic accident—obscures God's glorious design. These principles were foundational in the teachings of Stalin and Hitler.

This biography is the true story of a girl who learned ideologies from tyrants who killed millions. She grew up in Soviet Russia under Stalin. Her education was dominated first by the dogma of the Communist Party and later by the intense training of Hitler Youth. She believed what she was told to believe. Her Christian parents' message of God's love was silenced.

She lived through the destruction of her home and way of life. She survived harrowing evacuations, bombings, and deprivation as a refugee. Through it all, God preserved her life, but her heart turned away from her family's faith to search for happiness in the world. Still, God pursued, preparing her for the day when she would hear His voice.

The life of Anita Friesen began on the steppes of Ukraine and ended in America. This unusual story, full of adventure and danger, eventually led to a life of complete dedication and service to God. I knew Anita as my mother-in-law. Her intense passion for sharing the gospel left an indelible mark on me.

The details in this biography come from hours of interviews with Anita, combined with research into relevant historical background. She had a vivid memory, and I did what I could to include all she shared. I've extrapolated conversations and transitions as needed, but the stories belong to her.

As a child, Anita wasn't aware of her own historical context, but as a historian I like to fit things into the big picture. Background text has been added in italics, and I've also included a diagram of her large family because so many names can get confusing.

You may possibly see yourself in Anita's life. Maybe you also know those who have been indoctrinated by the world's message and turned away from their family's faith and love. May this story encourage you to be patient and pray. God has a way of quietly reaching for and preserving those He has called.

Chapter 1
Snow Peepers—1938

Anita carefully picked her way across the ice as quickly as she dared. It was March, and the lake was still frozen over, but there were weak spots. She listened for the telltale crackle sounds that signaled danger.

Up ahead, her brother Arnold scouted the ice. He was on skates and could quickly escape if the ice began to give way. There were two younger boys with him out on the lake. They lived at the nearby orphanage and were always hungry for adventure with the eleven-year-old Arnold.

"Go back home, Anita. Go play with your dolls and leave us alone," yelled Arnold. "It's too dangerous for a girl."

Not to be discouraged, Anita pretended she didn't hear. She wasn't about to be left behind. Sure, her mother had told her not to cross the lake, but it was so cold that Mother wouldn't so much as look outside. Besides, she knew her brother would watch out for her. He had to talk tough with his friends nearby, but once she made it part of the way across, he would make sure she was safe.

The steppes of Ukraine were a hazardous place in the winter. Food was scarce, and hungry wolves roamed the landscape. It was important for the children to stay together. Anita knew the danger, but, unlike the other girls in the village, she craved adventure. The possibility of an encounter with wolves just made her more determined to keep up with the boys.

This time, Anita had a goal: snow peepers. It was the season for the little white flowers to poke their heads from beneath the snow, just begging to be gathered. Her mother would not approve of her crossing the lake to the steppes, but she would be delighted with a bunch of flowers for the table. Anita didn't intend to tell her mother where she picked them.

It took about fifteen minutes to cross the ice. Finally, they climbed onto the bank and surveyed the grassland in every direction. There were no trees to hinder the view, just miles and miles of snow-covered plains. They took their time looking around. Squinting from the glare of the snow, Arnold carefully scanned for any gray-brown shapes moving across the ground in the distance. Anita knew that wolves would be unusual during daylight. They hunted mostly at night, sometimes even prowling through the village. The children were never allowed outside after dark in the wintertime, even in their own yards.

Arnold carried a big stick because it could look like a gun to the wolves. Since the group was bundled from head to toe against the cold, the wolves would not be able to tell that they were children. The pack would be cautious if they all stuck together.

With no wolves in sight, eight-year-old Anita became absorbed in her quest for snow peepers. "Stay close, Anita," Arnold said, as she ran from flower to flower.

Anita didn't hear it at first, but she froze as a long moaning howl bellowed across the steppes. It was difficult to know how far or how close the wolves might be, or even from what direction the sound came, but the children knew they had been spotted.

"Let's go!" Arnold shouted. The boys ran from whatever they were poking in a gully and Anita joined them, squealing with excitement. Clumped together, they hurried back, retracing their steps across the lake to the safety of their village.

As they left the lake, the children entered the lane leading into the village. There were houses on both sides and huge trees, stark and leafless, stretching over their heads. Doors and windows were all shut tightly against the cold, but the rising smoke from the chimneys was a welcome sight. Anita could smell the familiar odor of the burning cow chips that most villagers used for fuel. Her feet were beginning to ache from the cold. Mother had stuffed newspaper inside her boots, but the cold had gotten through. The warm hearth was calling. She looked forward to sitting on the long bench by the oven and leaning back on the hot bricks.

Arnold continued down the street with his friends, but Anita turned in at the gate to her home. After struggling with the heavy door and its frozen metal latches, she entered and began peeling off her heavy clothing. Her twin brother Rudolf, nicknamed Rudi, and younger sisters were playing with their toys in a corner, and her older brother Helmut was reading a book. It was early in the afternoon, so she knew that Mother was across the wagon road, helping her invalid grandmother.

The oven was stoked, the hearth spotless, and the kitchen smelled of borsch. It was a typical Mennonite household: orderly, well-stocked, and comfortable. The Friesens, Katharina and Gerhard, lived here with their six children and many chickens, pigs, dogs, rabbits, doves, and goats along with countless less-welcome creatures. Their Ukrainian home in the small Mennonite village of Franzfeld was under Joseph Stalin's control. The year was 1938.

***

In 1525, shortly after the start of the Protestant Reformation, Anita's ancestors migrated to Germany from the Netherlands where Mennonites could no longer purchase land or become citizens. However, they still faced increasing persecution. An answer to their situation came from Russia in a decree by the czarina Catherine II. Published in 1763, the manifesto invited foreign colonists to settle land recently taken from the Turks. The first Mennonite families began migrating in 1789, and by the mid-1800s, Mennonite colonies had formed just north of the Black Sea in southern Ukraine. The village of Franzfeld was established in 1869 as part of the Yazykovo colony, a rural settlement. By 1930, several hundred resided there.

The decades of freedom in Russia brought great prosperity to the hard-working Mennonites. Unfortunately, persecution began again when the land liquidation laws of 1915 were enacted. These laws required all property owners of German background to sell off their holdings within eight months. The penalty for refusal would be banishment to Siberia. In addition, nearly a decade of political unrest—including the aftermath of World War I, civil war, revolution, and the establishment of the Soviet government—brought about many changes. Now, the communist government ruled with an iron hand. Freedom of worship was no longer allowed. The villages were turned into "collectives" and private land was taken away. Religious and political suppression were enforced, and many faced imprisonment, exile, or execution for resistance.

Anita knew nothing of the troubles her family faced in 1938. More importantly, she did not know of a God who loved her. Her mother and father, though believers, were forbidden to share their faith. Anita had never seen a Bible or visited a church service. Her only witness was the example set by her parents and the beautiful creation she observed each day.

Map of Franzfeld

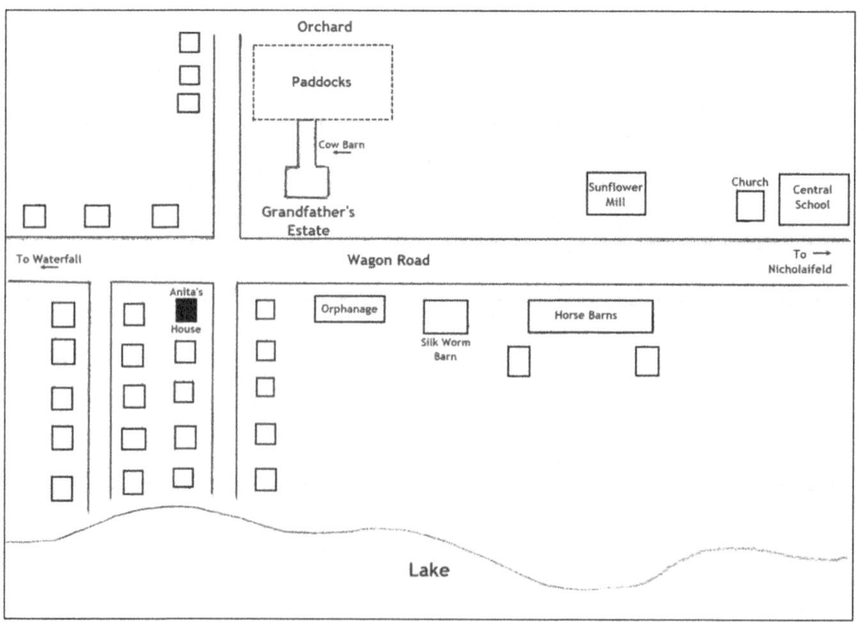

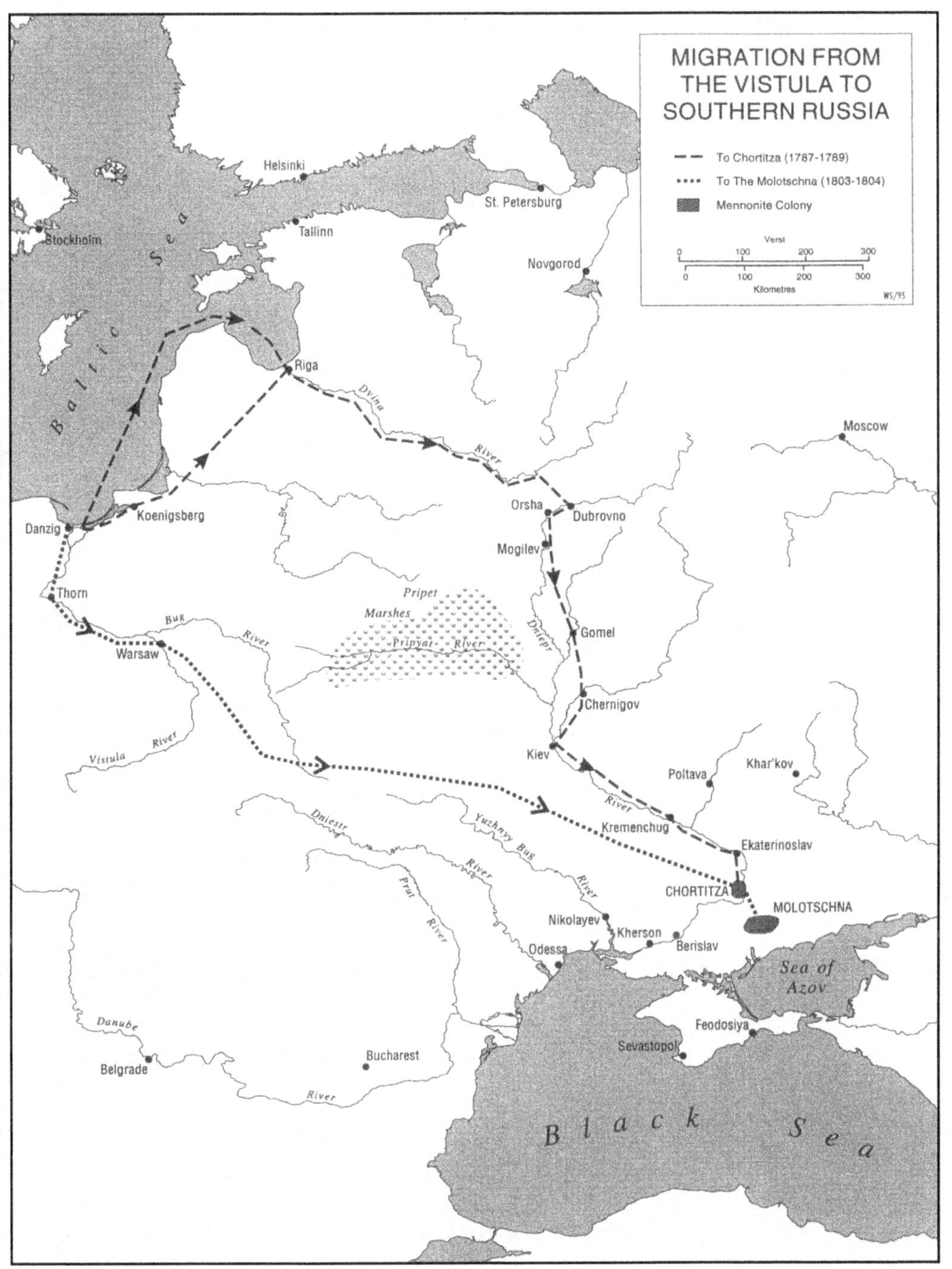

MIGRATION FROM THE VISTULA TO SOUTHERN RUSSIA
To Chortitza (1787-1789)
To The Molotschna (1803-1804)
Mennonite Colony
Verst
0 100 200 300
0 100 200 300
Kilometres
WS/95
Helsinki
St. Petersburg
Tallinn
Novgorod
Stockholm
Baltic Sea
Moscow
Riga
Dvina
River
Danzig
Koenigsberg
Orsha
Dubrovno
Mogilev
Thorn
Bug
River
Pripet
Marshes
Pripyat River
Dniepr
Gomel
Warsaw
Chernigov
Vistula
River
Kiev
River
Poltava
Khar'kov
Dniestr
Yuzhnyy Bug
River
Kremenchug
Prut
River
Ekaterinoslav
CHORTITZA
MOLOTSCHNA
Nikolayev
Kherson
Odessa
Berislav
Danube
Sea of Azov
Feodosiya
Sevastopol
Belgrade
River
Bucharest
Black Sea

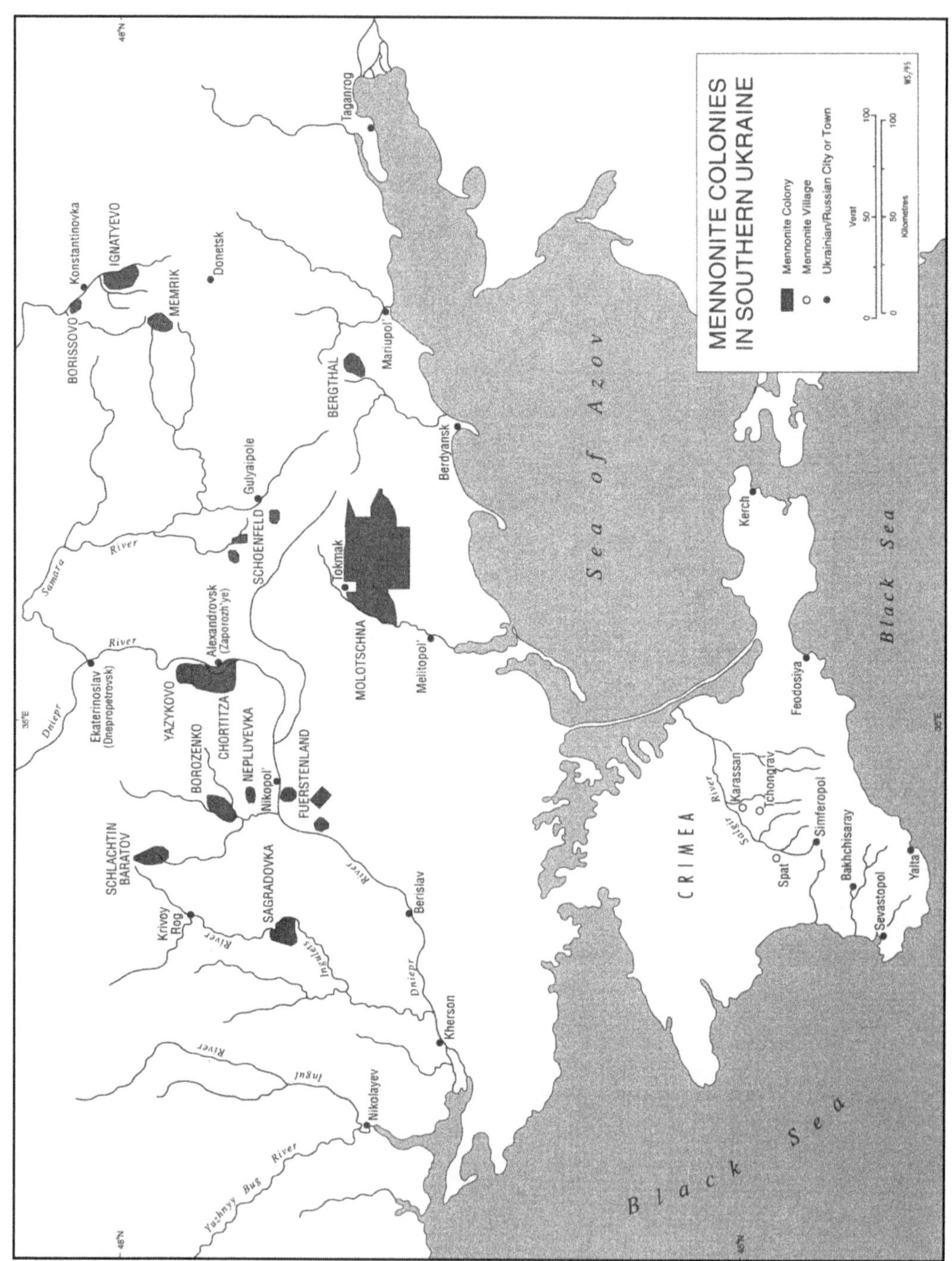
MENNONITE COLONIES
IN SOUTHERN UKRAINE
Mennonite Colony
Mennonite Village
Ukrainian/Russian City or Town
Verst
Kilometres
WS/95
Taganrog
Konstantinovka
IGNATYEVO
BORISSOVO
MEMRIK
Donetsk
BERGTHAL
Mariupol'
Berdyansk
Sea of Azov
Kerch
Black Sea
Gulyaipole
SCHOENFELD
Tokmak
MOLOTSCHNA
Melitopol'
Samara River
River
Dniepr
Ekaterinoslav
(Dnepropetrovsk)
Alexandrovsk
(Zaporozh'ye)
YAZYKOVO
BOROZENKO
CHORTITZA
NEPLUYEVKA
Nikopol'
FUERSTENLAND
SCHLACHTIN
BARATOV
SAGRADOVKA
Krivoy
Rog
Berislav
River
Dniepr River
Inhulets
River
Kherson
Ingul River
Yuzhnyy Bug River
Nikolayev
Black Sea
CRIMEA
River
Solgir
Karassan
Tchongrav
Spat
Simferopol
Bakhchisaray
Sevastopol
Yalta
Feodosiya
48°N
35°E
30°E
46°N

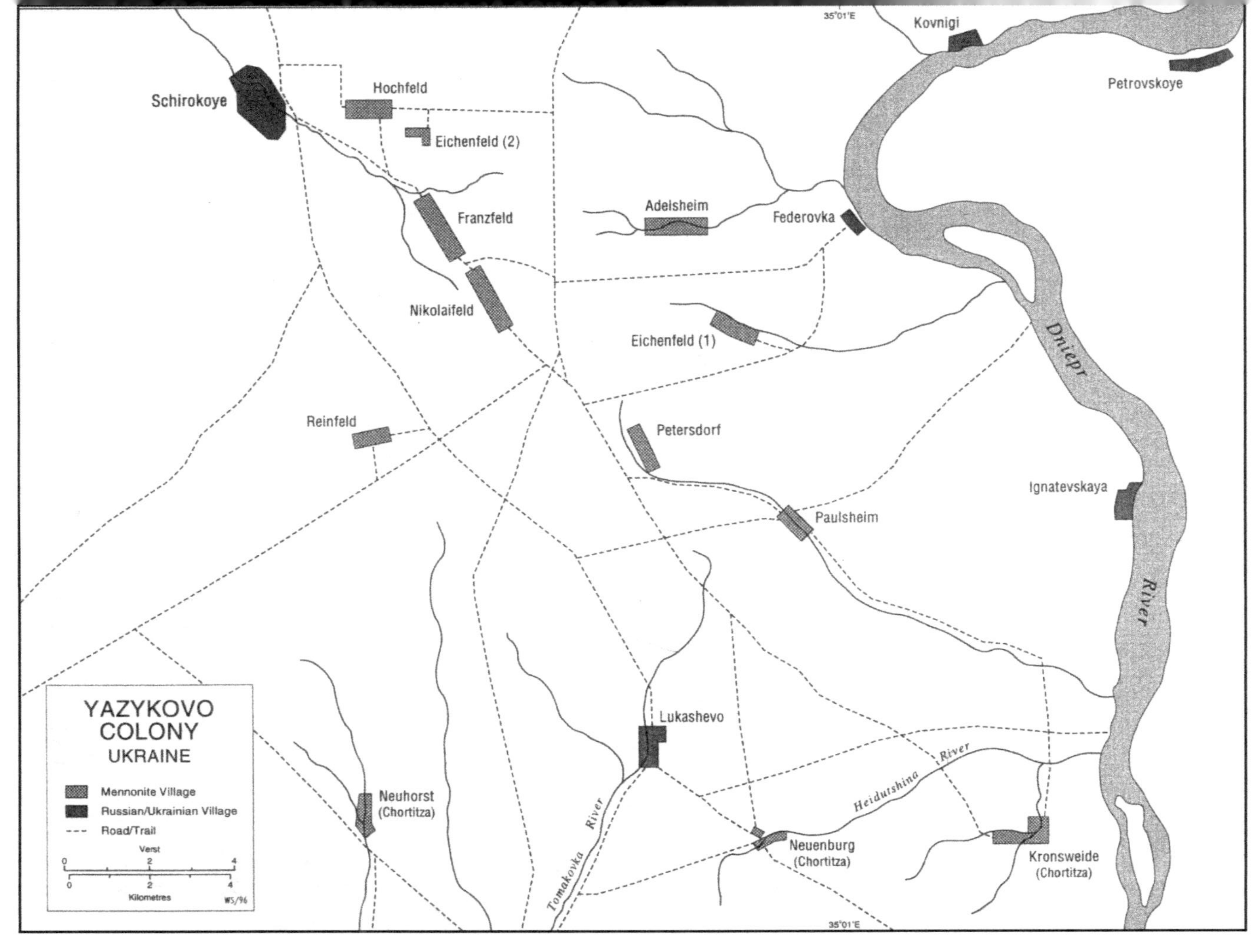

Schirokoye
Hochfeld
Eichenfeld (2)
Kovnigi
Petrovskoye
35°01'E
Adelsheim
Federovka
Franzfeld
Nikolaifeld
Eichenfeld (1)
Dniepr
River
Reinfeld
Petersdorf
Ignatevskaya
Paulsheim
Lukashevo
YAZYKOVO
COLONY
UKRAINE
Mennonite Village
Russian/Ukrainian Village
Road/Trail
Verst
0   2   4
0   2   4
Kilometres
WS/96
Neuhorst
(Chortitza)
Heidulshina River
Tomakovka River
Neuenburg
(Chortitza)
Kronsweide
(Chortitza)
35°01'E

Chapter 2
Soldiers in the Village

Anita's mother burst through the door.

"Helmut, quickly! Find the dog—the soldiers are coming!"

Helmut, Rudi, and Anita scrambled out of the house, scattering and shouting the dog's name. They had forgotten what day it was.

The children could hear the guns going off farther up the village. Arnold joined them, and they quickly found Julebars, their dog. The dog struggled to get away and run. He was already excited by the sounds of gunfire and the pandemonium of dogs barking and yelping in pain. Between the four of them, the children managed to get Julebars inside and then bolted the door.

Today was the terrible day that came every year. The communist soldiers came through the town and shot every dog they saw outside. They said they did it to stop rabies from spreading in the village. It was Soviet Russia's decree that on a certain day of the year, all dogs that were not indoors would be killed. Soldiers merrily carried shotguns through each village, laughing as they whistled hunting calls to lure dogs outside.

The soldiers came nearer as shot after shot rang out, and after that, yelping and whining.

Inside the house, Julebars cowered under the table. Suddenly, his fear and excitement peaked, and he charged across the room. Anita whispered "No!" but he took a mighty leap and crashed through the window. The glass shattered, the dog was through, and a soldier's shotgun erupted with a loud blast. The children saw Julebars collapse.

Angry and grieving, Anita wept as she stared out the broken window. Just a short distance away she could see the soft fur of her friend lying still, his chestnut coat stark against the blood-stained snow.

"Why?" Her voice was thick with pain. "Why do the soldiers have to be so mean? Julebars protected our family! Why are there so many awful rules?"

"Hush, Anita." Anita could tell Mother was angry, too, but she wouldn't dare say a word against the government. It was a dog this time. Next time, it could be worse.

Anita watched from the window as soldiers piled up dog carcass after dog carcass by the horse stables. She looked at Arnold. Julebars was his dog.

Hatred in his eyes, Arnold got up and left to get his dog's body. The government expected the owners to bury their own dogs. The frozen earth was an added cruelty. Arnold would be out there digging for hours.

Please, Anita thought. *Please, Arnold, don't say anything to the soldiers.*

At school they had been taught that no one was allowed to question the rules, and if they did, bad things would happen.

***

Franzfeld had not known many peaceful times. Persecution began under the tsarist regime. A few years later, Germany took over Ukraine during World War I. In 1918, the Germans withdrew, and a terrible time of anarchy erupted in the colonies. Bands of anarchists under the leadership of Nestor Ivanovich Makhno ravaged the countryside. The communist Red Army and the tsarist White Russian armies fought for control of the territory. Outlaws occupied many Mennonite towns, destroying some and murdering many villagers. One night in October 1919, Franzfeld was attacked. Eleven people were murdered by the marauding bands of anarchists.

By the end of 1920, the Red Army had gained control of the area. As the Soviet regime was established, the villages were collectivized. Private land was seized, and the government took over farms and businesses. Any political or religious resistance was severely punished. During the next few years, 85 villagers from Franzfeld would be exiled to Siberia. By the 1930s, the Soviets had gained strict control of village life.

Chapter 3
The Christmas Man

"Children, it's time. Get your coats on." Mother beckoned to Lene, Anita's little sister. "Bring me your hat and scarf."

She did not have to say it again or even speak louder than a whisper because the rest of the children were anxiously waiting. It was the night when the Christmas Man came. On this special evening, the Friesen family crossed the wagon road to visit Grandfather and Grandmother for Christmas Eve.

The Christmas Man had already visited their school. Each year, he brought brightly colored paper cones filled with nuts and candy for every student. But at Grandfather's house, the treats were even more generous, and there was a huge fir tree adorned by ornaments and candles.

They bundled up quickly, and with Father in the lead, the family stepped out into the night. There were no streetlights nor the faintest glow from windows. Every house remained tightly shuttered against the cold. The snow-covered ground reflected the light from a waning moon, and it was just enough to see the shadowy shapes of the trees and the gate that led to the wagon road. The air was crystal clear and biting cold. The snow crunched beneath their feet and glistened under a twinkling sky. No one said a word as they walked. How could they, with their scarves pulled tightly across their mouths?

Anita shivered as she hurried to keep up with her father and brothers. It was not the cold that made her tremble—it was anticipation… and just a little bit of fear. Father often warned them about wolves that entered the village on long winter nights, looking for anything or anyone careless enough to be alone in the dark. Heart thumping furiously, she peered in every direction, searching for hungry creatures slinking about. Katie, her youngest sister, whimpered from behind, pressing her face against Mother's shoulder as they brought up the rear of the marching, crunching troop.

Village house

Across the road, the high stone fence stood with the gate swung open. The giant chestnut trees that lined the fence lifted their bare branches in a ghostly welcome. As they approached the house, Anita listened to the faint lowing sounds coming from the cattle bedded down in the barn. She wondered if wolves were listening, too.

The cold was starting to penetrate the thick layers of Anita's heavy coat, so it was a welcome relief when Grandfather opened the door. He didn't smile, but that was not unusual; he never smiled. Yet, Anita noticed that even her mother's expression remained unchanged.

Grandfather, Cornelius Harder, was a tall, dignified man in his early 60s. A large, well-groomed mustache hid his smile—if there ever was one. His weathered skin told of years spent outdoors working on his farm. The children called him "Brumm Bear" in German. That title of "Growling Bear" suited him, but they dared not say it to his face.

For more than 20 years Cornelius Harder had seen little to make him smile. He lost his first wife after just a few years of marriage. As a young man, he served as a veterinarian for the Russian czar's horses and cattle, but his family lost land and wealth to the regime. Then, the communist revolution overturned the monarchy in 1917. The Soviet Revolutionary Council of peasants and workers ruled without restraint, demanding grain, livestock, and money from Cornelius and all the other landowners. Many of his hired servants turned against him, and his property was exploited and vandalized.

War across Ukraine followed in 1919 with successive waves of military occupation by brutal armies. Rebellious bands robbed, looted, and terrorized. Partisans of the anarchist Makhno threatened to execute Cornelius if he did not reveal where he had buried his money. Several times he fled into hiding to escape the marauding bands of outlaws. He saw many friends and family members murdered in Franzfeld and nearby villages, and he also witnessed terrible things happen to the Jewish people in his hometown of Judenplan.

Still, he was one of the fortunate ones. Perhaps because of his skill as a veterinarian, the Soviets who now ruled found him useful. When the village was collectivized, he was placed in charge of Franzfeld's cattle breeding operation. He was allowed to stay in his home and work on the farm that now

Grandmother and Brumm Bear

belonged to the Soviet government. He lived subject to Stalin's whim. Another purge could come at any time, exiling more men to Siberia for some made-up infraction or less-than-enthusiastic obedience. He had to be very careful about what he said around the grandchildren. He knew they were scrutinized at school for opinions learned from family.

Yet, even in these troubled times, he was grateful that his only daughter, Katharina, lived nearby with her husband and six children. It was with pleasure that he greeted the excited faces at his doorstep. The family hurried inside, the older children polite and restrained and the younger ones squealing in delight upon locating the giant evergreen tree standing in the corner. Anita watched breathlessly as Grandfather slowly lit the candles that were carefully placed among the sparkling ornaments. These treasured decorations, remnants of a more prosperous time, were off-limits to Anita and the other children.

After admiring the twinkling tree, the children each took a seat at the table. Anita knew she had to sit quietly while Grandfather's hired servant poured black Russian tea from the large brass samovar. This ornate device was only used on special occasions. Even more special was the lump of sugar and the single small slice of lemon on Anita's tea plate. A dish of cookies and small, sweet breads was passed around. Anita had watched her mother and the other women spend many hours preparing them for this momentous evening.

Then, with great ceremony, each child was given a beautifully decorated empty plate. These were set out on a table in another room to await the coming of the Christmas Man. Anita knew that—if he thought she deserved it—the Christmas Man would leave candy, nuts, and cookies on her plate to discover the next morning.

Soon, it was time to bundle up for the walk back to their house. The wind was brisk and tugged at their scarves, but excitement and anticipation kept the chill out as they trudged home. Tired as they were, sleep came quickly, and so did the morning. Once again, they bundled up and set out for Grandfather's house, this time squinting against the glare of the snow and shouting greetings to neighbors.

The children quieted as Brumm Bear opened the door. They knew the rules and had to be patient. One by one, each gave Grandfather a kiss on the cheek. This task was complicated by his gigantic mustache. Then, they recited a simple poem.

I wish, I wish,
Although I'm small and hardly know what to wish,
Someday I'll be bigger and know a better poem.

Then, slowly, oh so slowly, Grandfather lit the candles on the tree again as the children glanced excitedly toward the loaded plates in the other room. Anita couldn't see it, but she was sure a smile was hidden somewhere behind that mustache.

Finally, with a flourish, Brumm Bear dismissed the children to find their plates. Squealing and laughing, they tumbled over each other in a race to the other room. Just as they hoped, the plates were there, filled with homemade mint- and caramel-flavored candies. There were nuts of all kinds, some coated in sugar, along with glazed licorice cookies that tasted of peppermint and ginger. An enormous orange, rarely seen in Franzfeld, was a sweet surprise. On some plates there were mittens, socks or handkerchiefs, and special little toys. The Christmas Man really had been generous, and the children took careful inventory of each little present.

They shared teatime with the adults before heading home for more cookies and candies that Father had brought back from the city. Every year, he gave each of them a lemon—an unusual yet precious gift from a loving father. Sadly, he was not permitted to share the infinitely greater gift given by their heavenly Father long ago.

***

Gerhard, Katharina, and Cornelius longed for a different kind of Christmas. The Christmas Man was a pathetic substitute for the One they wished to celebrate. How they ached to share the truth with the children. But it was too risky. If they dared, the consequences would be exile, torture, or death, and then who would take care of their family? The truth would have to wait.

Chapter 4
Zcentralschule—1939

It was only about a half mile to the central school between Franzfeld and Nikolaifeld. Anita and her brothers walked there most days, even when the snow was piled up to the roof of their house. But in the spring, after the melt or a heavy rain, the wagon road became so muddy that it was impossible to arrive at school in acceptable condition. On those days, a wagon stopped by their gate and took them the short distance. It was absolutely necessary that the youth of Soviet Russia came to school with spotless clothes.

Anita loved going to school, and this was her last year as a Little Octobrist, a term referring to the Bolsheviks' October Revolution of 1917. So many exciting things happened at school. Of course, she was expected to work very hard at her lessons, and at times it was difficult to understand the Russian teachers, but the games were always fun. They wore bright red jumpers and enjoyed many outdoor activities.

The year before, she had been in a ballet class and performed for the whole school in a beautiful white costume.

While in kindergarten, the Mennonite children were allowed to speak Plattdeutsch, or Low German, at school just as they did

Gerhard (far left) and family in Nikolaifeld

at home, but at *Zcentralschule* only Russian was permitted. Anita did not mind learning Russian. She knew that if she did well, Stalin would be very proud of her, and she would be useful to the Soviet state. Every day she saw his picture and wondered what it would be like to meet him. She had been told that he loved children and especially wanted her to be happy.

***

Anita, like all the other children, did not realize it was Stalin's strategy to train children to love and obey the state. Children were to be treated as if they were very special to the Communist Party and represented a bright future. Stalin knew that education was the cornerstone for creating a new socialist society. He required that teachers present him as the hero of the revolution and role model for all children. Pictures depicted him as benevolent and god-like, encouraging obedience and hard work in school. The program was very effective, and the children grew to revere communism above all, even above their parents.

***

The state also prioritized the children's health, which was not as enthusiastically received. Once a month, Soviet officials came from the city to inspect the school and the village. As part of the initiative, a city nurse administered a large spoonful of cod liver oil to each child. The children were told to line up, hold their noses, and open their mouths as the nurse delivered the awful-tasting oil.

On those days, the children returned home to unusually quiet parents. The Soviet officials had also paid a visit to each house to inspect for anything that was considered unacceptable to the state, such as Bibles, crucifixes, or censured books. At Anita's house, a large banner with a red star would be hung on the living room wall. The Friesen home had been chosen to host the meetings of the Red committee. A red cloth covered the table, and a large picture of Stalin was prominently set up. In the evening, the door would close, and Anita knew she would not be allowed in that part of the house.

This afternoon, however, Anita was going to accompany her mother to visit Tjitka Marie in the nearby village. Tjitka Marie was a special friend. She had been nurse and governess to Anita's mother, and even now she worked for the family, helping with housework and cooking. Her husband, Uncle Jack Unum, worked as foreman for Grandfather. Anita wondered what her house would look like, since this was the first time she had been allowed to visit.

She shivered as they walked past the village cemetery. Anita had been there before, at Easter celebration and Day of the Dead. That was when the Russian villagers left decorated eggs and paska, a sweet bread baked in coffee cans, on the graves. She imagined what it was like at nighttime when the dead came out to eat the paska and eggs. Father told her that it wasn't the dead, but wolves from the steppes. That was almost as scary.

Tjitka Marie's house was a typical Ukrainian home, but Anita's eyes went immediately to an unusual display in the corner. There was a beautifully framed sculpture of a man hanging by his arms on wooden beams. She had never seen such a thing before. Why was that man there? Was he a criminal? She wondered if the Soviet officials had seen it. Would Tjitka Maria be in trouble?

It reminded her of another experience she had while visiting a friend. They were playing in the attic, and Anita opened one of the drawers in a stored chest. She saw a framed picture of a family dressed in royal clothes. The woman had a crown on her head, the man had medals on his jacket, and the daughters looked like beautiful princesses.

"We are never to open that drawer," Anita's friend whispered as she frantically slammed it shut. "You must not tell anyone what you saw."

Anita did not tell, and she would say nothing about Tjitka Marie's statue. But why wasn't Stalin there instead? What did it mean? She wanted to ask questions, but her friend's panic had taught her to be cautious. She knew that some things were forbidden and never to be discussed. Anita heard of neighbors who were banished for that very reason. The week before, Uncle Peter had been sent to live in Siberia. She did not know why, and her parents refused to talk about it.

After leaving Tjitka Marie's house, Anita and her mother walked back to Franzfeld in silence.

***

There was good reason to be silent. Katharina could sense Anita's unspoken questions as they headed home. She wanted to tell her many things, but she dared not. Life was difficult enough, and the smallest mistake could mean the exile of her husband. So many of the village men had been taken already. Gerhard managed to keep his job by cooperating, and she would not jeopardize that. Katharina understood how the children were pressured at school to report on their home life. Maybe things would be different someday.

Still, she was no stranger to hard times. Katharina Harder was born in 1905 in Kronsweide, Ukraine, to a wealthy Mennonite family. Her father, who would later be known as Brumm Bear, worked hard as the veterinarian for the czar's fine horses and cattle to provide for the family. Her life was simple and comfortable, with sixteen hired servants to attend to her needs.

But the relative peace of her early years was shattered with the sudden passing of her mother, followed by her father's remarriage. She was later sent to a boarding school, away from her dominant and abusive stepbrother, and it wasn't long before the October Revolution turned Ukrainian life upside down. When their hometown was destroyed by fire, Katharina's family relocated to Franzfeld. But it, too, experienced marauding bands that murdered and plundered throughout the fall and winter. The years that followed were marked by drought, famine, and a terrible epidemic of typhus that further ravaged the country.

In 1926, Katharina's parents arranged her marriage with Gerhard Friesen, a young veterinary student in the nearby village of Nikolaifeld. Having seen such misery and heartache, Katharina did not want to marry. But the decision was not hers to make, and thirteen years later, she was a mother to six children and a wife to a loving husband who had somehow managed to provide for his large family in very difficult circumstances.

Anita, of course, knew nothing of the horror that her mother endured as a teen. Like many children, she was satisfied with a warm house, a full plate, and loving parents. Thoughts of the future, or the past, did not trouble her.

Chapter 5
Summertime

School vacation and warm weather brought a season filled with exciting adventures to the children of Franzfeld. Of course, there was swimming and fishing in the lake, but one of Anita's favorite activities was catching crayfish.

First, she had to catch frogs. That required stealth. As the frogs sat on the bank, Anita quietly approached with a rock, smashing the nearest one. Just like the boys, she learned to yank their legs off to use for bait.

The children's best hunting spot was around the submerged roots of a large willow tree along the lake's edge. The willow's slender branches provided a shady habitat for the crayfish to thrive.

Anita and the others tied strings around the frog legs, attached the strings to a stick, and shoved the stick into a crevice under one of the half-exposed roots. In minutes, the crayfish latched onto the bait and, being the greedy creatures they were, wouldn't let go even as the children slowly pulled the strings up. Each time, Anita carefully pulled them away from the bait, squealing as their claws pinched her fingers.

After a few hours, the children had a full bucket and proudly presented it to their mother, who cheerfully threw the crayfish into a big cast-iron kettle and set it to boil on the fire. Anita watched while the gray-green creatures turned bright red in the heat. The highlight of the day came when Mother dumped out the steaming crayfish on the table. Much laughter and silliness accompanied this meal as the normally well-mannered family tore into the treat, ripping the crayfish limb from limb and tossing leftover shells at each other.

Franzfeld had quite a few enormous mulberry trees that were popular in the summer months. It was the season for mulberries, and the tall, heavy-limbed trees were perfect for climbing. Since the fruit was free to be picked, the children spent many hours climbing the huge trees and eating their fill. While the children enjoyed their sweet treat, the leaves of the mulberry tree were valuable to the village.

Just up the road from Anita's house stood a large barn that housed a silkworm facility. Each day, villagers collected mulberry branches to chop and spread in the various cubicles of the barn where the squirming silkworms dined. Once the leaves were devoured by the voracious worms, the villagers piled up the empty branches behind the building.

Occasionally, an adventurous silkworm that was attached to these discarded branches would escape. There was always one. Anita loved rummaging through the pile and taking the brave silkworm to live in a box in her room. She faithfully fed it mulberry leaves until it grew old enough to make a cocoon. Unlike its friends in the silkworm barn who were sacrificed for their silk, this one emerged as a beautiful silkworm moth.

One summer day, Anita and Rudi were climbing the mulberry trees in their grandfather's garden when Anna, a young Russian woman who worked in Brumm Bear's house, joined them. She loved the children and often played games with them, too.

But Anna was different. She was demon-possessed—at least, that is what the children were told. Her parents had been murdered during the turmoil that enveloped the town twenty years earlier, and Anna had survived by hiding for a month in the cellar of her home. The horror of it all left terrible scars on her soul. Although much loved by the villagers and treated with kindness, Anna often had fits of uncontrollable seizures that left her out of control. Sometimes, all at once, Anna would be overwhelmed and scream and strike at whatever she perceived was attacking her. Her body stiffened, her back hunched, and her face contorted as she flailed at the air, shouting, "Go away! Go away! Go away!"

On this particular day, she was high in the branches of a mulberry tree when a seizure began. Most of the children scattered, but Anita watched in horror and fascination as Anna stood up on a broad branch of the tree and began shrieking and punching the air, jolting about wildly. To everyone's amazement, Anna did not fall from the branch. She soon gained her composure and climbed down safely. Anita could only wonder how someone could survive such a situation. It was beyond her understanding whether something, if anything, was protecting her friend in that very moment, holding her up in that tree.

***

Each summer, the hunt for yellow-eared snakes drew the children to a waterfall at one end of the lake. There, the water spilled over an earthen dam, tumbling into a canyon filled with boulders, trees, and brambles. At the bottom was a deep green pool, thick with moss and algae. Nearly hidden by the thick underbrush and overhanging tree limbs, the grotto was dark, and the air smelled of moldy grass. The colors were so blurred by the shadows that it was hard to tell where the branches ended and the water began.

In this dingy oasis, the yellow-eared snakes thrived, slipping in and out of the pool and leaving narrow trails as they swam. They were slender black creatures with bright yellow stripes near their heads. The small, thin snakes were perfect for hiding in a pocket to be suddenly pulled out and make the girls scream—except Anita, who was unafraid of snakes and therefore unlikely to panic. She wanted to catch them herself, following the boys to the canyon's edge. However, the descent into the dank and swampy canyon was too intimidating. That part of the adventure she left to the older boys. But she was delighted to join in the pranks and watch her friends squeal.

Occasionally, the boys managed to ditch little Anita, but she always found adventure on her own. One day, she set out on a secret mission. "Who needs boys?" she said to herself, running up the road that followed the hedge along her grandfather's property. Almost out of breath, she turned the corner around the backside of the estate. Quickly checking to see if anyone was looking, she dropped down by the hedge.

At the base of the eight-foot hedge was a small dog tunnel, almost completely hidden by tall weeds. Sharp twigs snagged her hair and scratched her face as she crawled through. Her goal was Brumm Bear's forbidden orchard. Anita was not allowed in this wonderful place by herself, although she could not understand why. She had been in the orchard many times during harvest with her family, so she saw no reason not to be there now.

Just don't get caught, she thought to herself. *Don't make any noise and stay in the shadows.*

Grandfather's farm was one of the biggest in the village. The house was a large stone structure that, like all the village houses, was attached to an animal barn. His barn was particularly big because the Soviet cattle operation was housed on his land. Beyond the barn were corrals—one for the cows and another for the calves.

Past the corrals was a large fenced area for the vegetable garden. Even farther back, and away from the workers who tended the cattle, lay the beautiful, secluded orchard. Here, giant walnut and hazelnut trees dominated with huge limbs drooping to the ground. The orchard also abounded with fruit trees of plum, cherry, pear, and apple, but it was the immense walnut tree near the edge of the orchard that enchanted Anita. Its thick branches reached all the way to the ground. Dark and tangled, they encircled the tree and formed a room. Inside was a secret place where glimmers of light made leopard spots on the damp ground and a little girl was free to dance about or play quietly. No one could see her as she peered out from behind the branches to watch the activity on the farm.

It was important to keep an eye out for anyone coming close. If someone saw her, or worse, Aza the dachshund started barking, Brumm Bear was sure to find out. Then, she would be in trouble, although she had never been caught and had no idea what that might mean.

Even the calves in the nearest corral were a threat. If one of them saw movement in the orchard, curiosity would bring the whole bunch closer. A spooked calf would cause them all to scamper, alerting other cows nearby. This had the potential to raise a ruckus, and then everyone on the farm would know something—or someone—was in the orchard. Nevertheless, Anita settled behind the wall of leaves and began to fill her apron with nuts off the damp ground, nervously imagining all sorts of consequences. If she was lucky, she could sneak the walnuts out of the orchard and crack them open. It wasn't hard to hit them with a rock and break the shells. Some of the nuts would be ripe and tasty.

Anita did not stay long. It was too risky. She looked around and, keeping to the shadows, crept back toward the hedge. Suddenly, she heard a single bark. The sharp-eyed Aza had noticed her movements, and it was just enough to raise the alarm. There were only moments before the little sentry would launch into a frenzy of barking and charge Anita's direction. In a panic, Anita raced to the hedge and dove through the tangle of branches.

Once back on the road, the danger was over and Aza gradually quieted down. Anita skipped toward home, triumphant that she had once again faced the challenge and gotten away with it. Grinning to herself, Anita decided she would not even tell her twin brother, Rudi, about her visit to the secret hideout.

Chapter 6
Secrets

It seemed like everybody had secrets in Franzfeld. Often, Anita overheard her mother and father talking in serious tones, but the conversation stopped when she approached. Yet, even at her age, she could see the dark shadows of worry in their eyes and sense the fears they would not share.

Her father worked every day as a veterinarian at the Soviet horse breeding farm in Franzfeld. The beautiful mares and proud stallions were some of the best in the country, bred to provide mounts for officers in the Red Army. Sometimes, Anita and Rudi would sneak behind the barn, climb up, and peer over the barn windows to watch the men working with the stallions. This was forbidden for the children, but she knew her father wouldn't punish her. He treated her more gently than her brother, calling Anita his *liebling* (darling).

But even here, she knew there were secrets. Every now and then, she saw her father talking quietly with her uncle Abraham, then suddenly turn and pretend to be working when a third person approached.

✳✳✳

Anita's father knew that even in Franzfeld, secrecy meant survival. Gerhard Friesen was born in the nearby village of Nikolaifeld in 1901 to a wealthy landowner. When the communists took over, his family's land was collectivized, and because of their position, they all suffered. Gerhard's brother Peter, a scientist, was killed by the Soviets. Two brothers-in-law were arrested, sent to Siberia, and never heard from again.

Gerhard survived by studying to become a veterinarian. He proved useful to the Soviet cause and managed to keep his family safe. Still, there was always the fear that he would come under suspicion. It was not uncommon for another villager to tell the secret police some information just to gain a favor for their own family.

Family of Peter Friesen, Gerhard on left

Gerhard's home in Nikolaifeld

Chapter 7
Stalin Youth—1940

"Be prepared," Anita commanded with her arm raised high in a salute.

"Always prepared!" shouted Rudi as he stood at attention facing her.

Today was the first day of *Zcentralschule*, and the twins were practicing the greeting that would be required as they entered the building. At ten years old, all children became Young Pioneers. They had already received their uniforms and were proudly dressed, waiting for inspection from their brother Helmut. He was older and knew what was expected.

Anita fussed with the bright red scarf around her neck. It was held by a silver clip stamped with a burning red flame and the words *budye-hatov*, which meant "Be prepared, always prepared."

Her white blouse and black skirt were spotless. She eagerly imagined standing and saluting the others in her class. All Young Pioneers were instructed to stand tall and proudly salute all other students who wore the uniform. She reminded herself that she could not giggle or laugh when in school. A Young Pioneer had to be dignified and always act politely. She already memorized the first rule of a Young Pioneer:

"It is the duty of each school child to acquire knowledge persistently so as to become an educated and cultured citizen and to be of the greatest possible service to his country."

She began softly singing a song she learned in school last spring.

Hammer, sickle, Soviet star,
All the little children

Love it so, love it so.

Anita frowned as her mother spoke to her in Plattdeutsch. After all, Young Pioneers were only to speak Russian. She wanted to do her best in school, and obedience to Stalin and her teachers was very important. What would happen if her mother never learned to obey the government? Would Mother be in trouble too? Many family members had been sent away, and Anita worried that her family was not doing enough to obey the rules.

Today, each new Pioneer would be required to take an oath of allegiance. Anita had worked hard to recite the pledge accurately and boldly.

"I, Friesen, Anita, joining the ranks of the Vladimir Ilyich Lenin All-Union Pioneer Organization, in the presence of my comrades, solemnly promise: to passionately love and cherish my Motherland, to live as the great Lenin bade us to, as the Communist Party teaches us to, as require the laws of the Pioneers of the Soviet Union."

***

Zcentralschule was an impressive three-story brick building that stood between Franzfeld and Nikolaifeld. Its floors gleamed with polished tile, and the white walls were decorated with beautifully colored

Zcentralschule

posters of happy children and a smiling, kind-eyed Stalin. Red banners greeted the new students, and the atmosphere was electric with enthusiasm and pride. The hum of student voices was constantly punctuated with bold salutes of "Be prepared, always prepared!"

In the classroom, the atmosphere held a sense of quiet dignity. Anita knew that if she misbehaved, she would be punished sharply and embarrassed in front of her friends. Young Pioneers were never to disappoint, and she intended to be a good one. She was a good student, believing that one day, she, too, would be important and serve her country well. She would always be prepared to serve, fight, or die for the state, just like Stalin wanted.

But beyond the walls, the conversation was different—especially down by the outhouse. Youth from around the area, including Russians, Ukrainians, and Mennonites, all attended the *Zcentralschule*. Problems were unavoidable, and fights among the teenagers were an everyday occurrence.

"*Nyence kartoschka*," taunted the Russian boys. "German potato heads."

The Mennonite boys chanted back, "*Ruskie, puskie, keilbassa yedgyt, kony bez chjosta, kony nyet chorditza.*" In English this meant, "Russian, Prussian, rides a horse with no tail, and doesn't know which way to go because he can't tell the head from the tail."

Arnold was always in the thick of it. He had a quick temper and a ready fist, much to his parents' disapproval. Anita watched and cheered when he tangled with the Russian boys, landing more than his share of punches. She wanted to join in, but she wasn't sure why she was supposed to fight with the Russian children or why they disliked her brother and called him names.

***

Mennonites had always been peaceful and committed to nonviolence. They believed in accepting whatever government God allowed to be in control. There was some resistance to the Soviet rule, but for the most part, the Mennonite colonies resolved to obey and honor what God had ordained for their country.

However, the Mennonite people's ethnic heritage drew suspicion of their possible allegiance to Germany. The German dictator, Adolf Hitler, came to power in 1933, and it became obvious to the Soviets that he wanted to control Ukraine. For this reason, all Mennonites and others of German background were suspected of being German spies. That decade saw many killed and thousands sent to Siberian labor camps.

Children, on the other hand, were taught to reject their family values and allegiances, giving all loyalty to the Soviet state instead. Even so, as in every generation, ethnic differences engendered hatred and, consequently, fights down by the outhouse.

Editor's note: The Russian words in this chapter were based on Anita's memory.

Chapter 8
A Soviet Celebration

Most weeks passed uneventfully, but on certain days the children looked forward to exciting celebrations. Today was one of them.

First, they saw a picture show in the big building next door to the school. It was called a theater, but Anita had been told that it used to be a church where her parents and the other Mennonite villagers used to meet once a week. She did not know what they had done there or why they had gone.

The Soviets transformed it into a theater that showed propaganda films to the children. Terrifying stories of war made lasting impressions, and the consequences for disloyalty to the state were made brutally clear.

Anita entered the theater with cheerful anticipation, but inside she felt uneasy. Most of the movies were interesting stories about brave soldiers who fought for the Soviet army, like the fearless Red commander, Kliment Voroshilov. Hearts bursting with pride, the whole theater sang along as the loudspeaker played the familiar ballad about his victories.

Other times, sad or frightening movies were on the screen. Last month, her heart was scarred. She watched soldiers throw babies into a bonfire. The distraught parents—rebellious villagers—helplessly stood by, screaming and weeping. Why the soldiers did this, she did not know, but it filled her with fear to know that they could.

But today, the movie was about a young Russian hero. Anita's eyes were glued to the screen during the story of a courageous Russian boy named Pavlik Morozov, the leader of the Young Pioneers in his school. His family lived in a village of landowners who refused to turn their property over to the government and join the collective. They were kulaks, or higher-income farmers, and she knew that her teachers called the kulaks "enemies of the state."

The film told how Pavlik's father had forged documents and sold them to bandits. Because of his loyalty to the Communist Party, Pavlik, at age 13, turned his father over to the secret police. His father was sent to a labor camp and later executed. Sadly, Pavlik's grandparents and uncle then brutally murdered the boy and his younger brother. Pavlik was hailed as a martyr and hero of the Young Pioneers.

Anita blinked back tears as she thought of how Pavlik died. How awful to be killed by your own family! She knew that she needed to be a loyal Pioneer but couldn't imagine turning her father in to the authorities. She had seen the poster in the school hallway with Pavlik's picture and knew of his statue in the city. Anita wished she could be that brave and important, but she loved her father, and the thought of him being executed terrified her. Her father's brother had been taken by the police. What had he done? Chills ran up her back as she remembered them whispering together. Would they take her father? What if he did something bad? What would she do?

Right after the film, Anita and her class marched out to the large open area in the schoolyard. In the middle was a great fire pit enclosed with low concrete blocks in the shape of a five-point Soviet star. A low hush fell over the crowd as the wood was lit and the flames reached higher and higher. Then, dancers appeared, dressed as Russian Cossacks. Bright-colored streamers followed them as they danced wildly around the fire, and the children clapped and sang along. A popular Soviet song blared through the loudspeaker while the young people from the city entertained. The energy of the crowd rose and crackled just like the sparks that rose from the bonfire. As the young performers shouted their enthusiastic praise of the Soviet state, the children jumped and cheered.

Gradually, the fire and the excitement died down. As the smoke cleared, the students trailed away, but the thrill lingered. They whispered to each other, speaking with the same desire: "I'll be there one day! Dancing with them, singing with them!" The students all felt it—a bond of unity, a shared determination to do all things to serve the beloved Stalin.

Chapter 9
Autumn

The cellar was a dark, cold room situated beneath the house, and it often fell to Anita to retrieve whatever her mother required for the next meal. The journey was an adventure. Harvest time had passed, and the cellar was crammed with all kinds of food that would feed the family through the long winter. It was also filled with all kinds of creatures seeking to eat their fill. Rodents of various sizes called it home, but so did the big snake that her father put there to keep the rat population under control. There were also a couple of hedgehogs stationed in the cellar to eat insects and mice.

Anita lifted the large door that covered the entrance and hooked it to the wall. Holding a lantern, she carefully stepped down the five wooden planks that served as stairs. A chill ran up her back as cold air carried the familiar scent of dirt, vinegar, and rat droppings to her nose. Off to her left were the big barrels of pickled watermelon, sauerkraut, and green tomatoes. There were other barrels of apples, apricots, and pears nearby. Crates of potatoes stood along the wall, and baskets of carrots, turnips, and many other supplies filled the shelves. Prepared jars of raspberry jam, pickles, and meats lined up like fat soldiers on the top shelf, ready to attack.

This time Mother wanted a jar of apricot jam. Slowly, Anita picked her way to the shelf, taking time to locate and avoid the big snake. Reading the jar labels by lantern light was not easy, especially when she needed to look between the jars for whiskers and little twitching noses peeking out.

Finally, she found the jam. Reaching slowly so as not to frighten some sleeping rodent, she drew it out from among its comrades. A flurry of activity from behind the jars startled her, but it was only a hedgehog. It made funny little noises as it resettled a few feet away. The scurrying noises had alerted the ever-vigilant snake, and as she retraced her steps, she saw him slithering between the barrels close to the stairs. With one last leap, she jumped to the steps, almost upsetting the lantern.

Having faced the dangers of the dark dungeon and emerging victorious, Anita proudly presented the trophy to her mother, who took it entirely unceremoniously. Then, she sent Anita to the big flour bin. Now this was an adventure of another kind!

The big flour bin was right off the warm kitchen and easy to reach. Anita obediently complied, lifting the big, slanted lid and scooping up some flour. This was a simple task during the daytime, but at night it was treated as a conquest. When the kitchen was dark, the bin was a favorite haunt of tiny mice. Children would quickly lift the lid as mice scampered in all directions, leaping out of the bin like grasshoppers. It was a test of reflexes to see how many mice could be slapped as they scrambled out. However, Anita's mother frowned upon this activity because it left yellow lines throughout the bin (evidence of frightened mice) and spoiled the flour.

Their house was a comfortable home made with thick adobe walls and picturesque wooden shutters. The barn joined the house at one end so the animals could be cared for during the winter when it was too cold to venture outside. It was divided into two halves with stalls for cows, goats, and horses. An attic above the house provided room to hang laundry and store supplies, serving as a quiet place for Anita to play with her dolls.

Between the kitchen and the barn were stairs leading to the cellar followed by another set that climbed to the barn's loft where hay was kept. At the top of these stairs, the family's doves nestled in niches with holes open to the outside. Just below the dovecote, pigs shared a pen with a multitude of unwelcome rats. There was a broom conveniently placed at the stall door, kept handy for chasing away the rats at feeding time.

Inside the house, a long brick oven opened into the kitchen and extended through the length of the home, warming all the rooms during the long winters. But there was one small room just off the kitchen that was kept cold and dark. It was used for storing bread, cookies, and other tempting items. Occasionally there was a basket filled with holiday candy kept just out of reach.

Sometimes, when Mother was across the road at Grandfather's, Anita and Rudi would sneak into the cold room, stack up chairs, and steal a few pieces of the forbidden candy. This adventure was not without consequences. Anita never forgot the day her older brothers ran screaming from the cold room in terror. Knowing the boys were plotting a candy raid, Anita's mother hid in a corner of the room wearing Father's long fur coat. Just when the boys were about to reach the candy, she let out a low wolf growl and shifted her fur coat. Chairs tumbled and the boys flew from the room terrified. For days, laughter greeted them as the story got around to family and friends.

Autumn also brought great thunderstorms. The weather could change quickly, and storms across the steppes took on fierce proportions. With few natural features to blunt the force of the wind, the little village often suffered from the effects of nature. One year, the giant chestnut tree that stood outside the family's house was uprooted, barely missing their home as it fell. From that time on, Anita's mother insisted that the children sleep under the sturdy oak table in the kitchen when it stormed. Adobe walls were known to collapse from high winds, and the strong legs of the table offered some protection. They were under that table a lot. Anita felt safe there, like a soldier in a stronghold, even during the frequent earthquakes.

One stormy night late in the season, a family of gypsies appeared at the door begging for shelter. It was not unusual to see gypsies come through the town, but they had a reputation for stealing, so most villagers avoided them. Anita heard rumors of gypsies stealing young children and staining their skin with walnut juice to make them unrecognizable. Many villagers feared the gypsies' revenge if they felt mistreated.

Because of the terrible weather, Anita's mother agreed to let the gypsy family shelter in the house with the condition they stay in the kitchen. Grateful to be out of the rain, the gypsies agreed, but Anita's family

Gypsies

spent a restless night worrying about the risk.

The next morning, when Anita's mother made bread, she offered the gypsies a loaf but kept the second one in her hands, intending to save it for her family. One old gypsy woman leaned over and spat on the loaf. Without any more hesitation, mother handed the second loaf over, and the gypsy group went on their way.

The Friesen Homestead

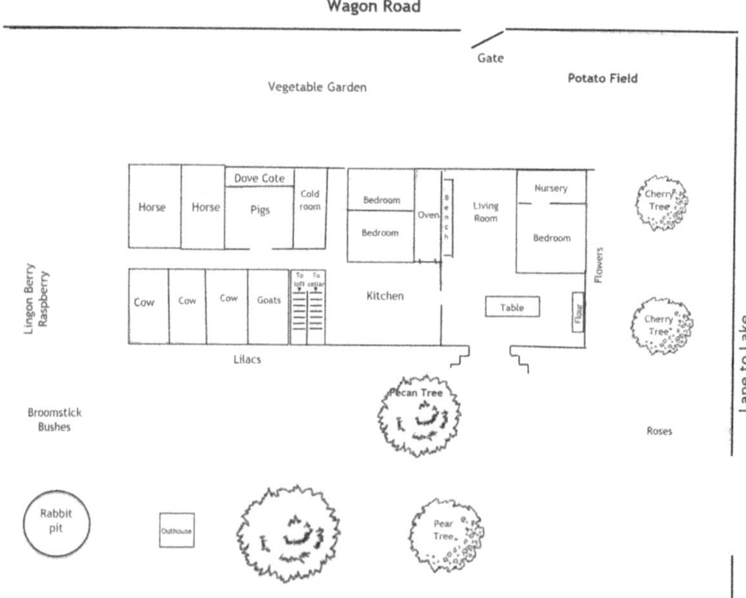

Chapter 10
Winter on the Ukrainian Steppes

Winter always came early to the steppes of Ukraine. Snow piled up to the eves of the houses, making it far too cold to venture outside. However, Anita's house stayed warm as long as a fire was maintained in the long brick oven. On cold evenings, it was particularly nice to sit on the long bench that ran alongside the oven. Often Father would read a book out loud or tell stories to the children as they snuggled up against the warm bricks.

Of course, it was much too chilly to take the short trip to the outhouse. Besides, wolves roamed the area at night. The barn was the convenient solution to that necessity, but it was not much warmer there, and it was always very, very dark.

One frigid evening, the mischievous Anita determined to play a trick on her twin brother. Rudi had made a trip to the barn and was finding a spot along the drainage ditch. Anita quietly followed, crawling along in the dark to scare him. Just at the worst moment for Rudi, she howled. Rudi jumped up and ran yelling that a wolf was in the barn. Anita screamed too, but she suddenly realized she would be spanked if their mother knew what she had done. Grabbing Rudi, she told him not to scream. Rudi quieted down, but he wouldn't speak to her for days.

Some Sundays, when the weather wasn't quite so bad, the family crossed the road to Grandfather's for afternoon tea. While the adults sat and talked, the children were sent to a small room adjacent to the barn where they were told to play quietly and not disturb the adults. Unfortunately, Anita was not one to play quietly.

Barn connected to house

The room opened onto a short hallway with stairs leading into the barn. Under the stairs, Aza the dachshund tended her litter of puppies. Just beyond, on the right side of the narrow barn aisle, were three fierce bulls chained by the snout to their stalls. There were cows and calves in stalls on the left.

"I dare you," Anita said one afternoon to Rudi and the other children, "to run up the aisle to the other end and back."

The others knew better, but Anita had to first prove that she was brave enough to do it herself. Taking a deep breath, she charged up the steps, infuriating Aza, who began barking furiously and nipping at her heels. Upset by the noise, the bulls lunged in their stalls, clanging their horns against the iron bars and bellowing wildly. Anita, trembling, reached the end of the long aisle and looked back, but all the other children had disappeared. Terrified by the noise but more afraid of the consequences from her parents, she turned and sprinted to the other side, past the roaring bulls and furious dog.

As her mother and uncle came to see what was happening, Anita and the children quickly sat down and pretended nothing was wrong, all smiles and sweet faces, yet quivering inside. Anita's mother looked at her suspiciously but said nothing. Uncle Abraham, on the other hand, grinned at her.

Uncle Abraham was a favorite among the children. He played along with their silliness and often joined in the fun. Years ago, Anita's mother had taken him in as a two-year-old orphan. Now, he was married, and his children were considered cousins. They lived in a small house on Grandfather's farm, and Uncle Abraham worked at the horse barn with Anita's father.

One day, he decided to bring his own bit of mischief. Taking the children outdoors, he harnessed up a pair of horses to the sleigh, loaded them inside, and turned the reins over to Helmut. All went well at first, but the horses were young and fiery, and Helmut

Sleigh ride

was only 13. As the horses quickened their pace, Helmut struggled to maintain control. It only seemed to make them go faster. Thinking the sleigh would tip, Anita panicked. She jumped out as the sleigh slowed at a turn, tumbling over and over in the snow. Helmut eventually managed to restrain the horses and circle back safely, leaving Anita humiliated in the snowdrift. She was almost frozen by the time she walked back to the house, yet she could not help but notice the amusement on Uncle Abraham's face.

Chapter 11
War on the Horizon

Spring had finally arrived, the snow peepers had come and gone, and the steppes of Ukraine were alive with wildflowers and new grass. Happy to finally be outside, Anita celebrated by climbing high up the huge pear tree that stood in her yard. Surrounded by the wonderful smell of pear blossoms, she perched on a limb and looked out across the lake to the steppes. It was an endless stretch of plains as far as the eye could see. There was nothing else.

All that interested her was right below in the surrounding village, and she wasted no thought on what she could not see. She had visited the Russian village nearby and taken one trip to visit her mother's family in Kronsweide, but it was also a small town and not very different from her own. She had seen pictures of Russian cities and other faraway places, but it was difficult to imagine anything other than the familiar rural countryside, its ordinary people, and their normal jobs and activities.

A faint buzz caught her attention. It sounded unfamiliar, not like an insect or farm machine. High in the tree, she looked every direction as the sound grew louder. Below her, she saw others pausing and gazing upward, hands shielding their eyes against the sun. Anita searched the sky and located a small object above the far end of the lake. It was yellow! Suddenly, she realized what it was. She had seen pictures of machines that could travel in the air, but she never expected to see one.

As it drew closer, she could hear the motor distinctly. Then, she could see yellow wings with black stripes and make out the head of the pilot. She watched as the plane flew the length of the lake, circling over the town. A few moments later, it turned and headed back the direction it came from. Delighted, Anita shouted down to her family gathered in the yard. She saw her little sisters jumping around with excitement. Quickly, she climbed down to join the others. Rudi, Helmut, and her little sisters Katie and Lene were all laughing and talking, sharing what little they knew of airplanes. Strangely, the men were excited too, but they were not laughing—nor were they smiling.

Life in the village of Franzfeld changed that day. When evening came, the men of the village gathered. For the children, the enthusiasm died away, replaced by an uneasy silence as the adults whispered among themselves. The next morning, Father and Arnold began digging a large hole in one corner of the yard. They called it a shelter but would not explain what it was for.

Chapter 12
Invasion

Everyone was anxious in Franzfeld. Everyone, that is, except Anita. Summer was coming, and she looked forward to the adventures ahead.

"Why are you digging that hole?" Anita asked Helmut. "Is it for more rabbits?"

It was a logical conclusion because Father kept a colony of rabbits within a deep earthen pit in their yard. The hole was about eight feet deep and fifteen feet across. Hay and fresh grass were thrown in for the rabbits' feed and bedding. The rabbits dug dens inside the walls for nests, but they couldn't burrow deep enough to escape. When Mother wanted some fresh meat for a stew, Helmut put down a ladder, climbed in, and chased down an unlucky rabbit. Anita would watch him as he killed it, putting her hands over her ears in case it screamed.

"No," Helmut said in answer to her question. "This is going to be a bomb shelter."

"What's a bomb?" asked Anita.

Helmut tried to explain. "An army is coming, and when it gets close, planes will come and drop bombs. We'll need a place to hide underground."

She wondered why they couldn't just get under the table like they did during thunderstorms. How bad could an army be? *Never mind,* she dismissed the thought. *Helmut is just grumpy.* Anita scampered off to see what her new baby brother was doing. She heard him crying and knew Mother would welcome her help.

The new baby was named Hansi. Born at the end of June, he was just a few weeks old. Anita hoped he would live longer than Peter, who was born two years before but had only lived a short time. She knew Mother was being extra careful with Hansi. Father wanted to have more children because the government would give them some money if they had eight children. That was fine with Anita because she loved dolls and was sure that someday she would want to have babies of her own. It was the duty of every Young Pioneer girl to raise children for the Soviet state. She would be proud to do her duty.

As Anita entered the house, she saw Father hanging the big red flag with the star in the living room. That meant there was going to be a meeting in the house later that evening. Anita started to ask him a question but hesitated when she saw the worried look on his face. She turned to go to the bedroom. There, her mother was feeding Hansi. When Anita approached, she noticed tears on her face. Without a word, her mother motioned for her to leave. Quickly, she hurried out, wondering why everyone was acting so strangely.

****

On June 22, 1941, Hitler's German army began a march to the east, invading Ukraine on its way to Moscow. Hitler's original plans called for much of the Ukrainian population's extermination with the rest deported to Germany for slave labor. The fertile lands of Ukraine were to be taken from the native Slavs and given to German settlers to farm, feeding the new German nation.

There was little resistance from the Soviets as huge territories of Ukraine were captured. City after city was bombed, invaded, and conquered by the German front moving steadily eastward. Stalin and the Soviet government, determined to leave nothing for the Germans, implemented a "scorched earth" policy. Mennonite villagers were ordered to evacuate ahead of the advancing army, and all crops and fields were torched. However, the German army moved faster than the evacuees. Some groups were overtaken and sent back to their villages to remain under German occupation.

Chapter 13
Evacuation

It was barely twilight when Anita awoke to the sound of gunfire. Her first panicked thoughts flew to her dog. *Were the soldiers shooting the village dogs again?* But there were so many voices shouting, and the footsteps of her brothers running through the house told her something bad was happening. Quickly, she climbed down from the bed she shared with her sisters, Lene and Katie. The little girls sat up in bed with terrified expressions on their faces. Running to the window, Anita pressed her face to the glass.

The street was filled with people. Neighbors ran back and forth, wagons hurried up and down the road, and horses plunged and reared in panic as their handlers attempted to harness them. There were soldiers shouting and waving their rifles. A staccato burst of gunfire sent panicked mothers screaming in all directions as one soldier pointed his rifle skyward and shouted.

"Quickly, girls," Father yelled as he entered their room. "Grab your clothes and get to the wagon." He hurriedly picked up two-year-old Katie as Anita and Lene scrambled to find their day dresses. Anita reached for her favorite doll, but her father shook his head.

"Go, there's no time for that." He shoved her to the door. Outside, Anita stopped. Dogs barked as the shrill voices of mothers rang out sharply, trying fiercely to manage their confused and crying children. All around there was shouting. Anita had never experienced such a frantic scene, and she stood, frozen, on the steps of her house. For a moment she wanted to run back inside, but then her father shouted, and her frightened feet responded.

Alarmed, the girls ran to the wagon. Mother was already on board, consoling her infant, who cried to be fed. Arnold and Helmut struggled to control the panicked horse. Rudi stood stiffly in the wagon, immobile amid the chaos surrounding him.

Soldiers moved along the street, shouting angrily and shoving anyone who was not in place. The soldier nearest their wagon raised his rifle and fired. Katie and Lene screamed in panic. Anita clapped her hands over her ears, trying desperately not to cry as the horse reared, nearly throwing Arnold to the ground. Then, the soldier shouted the order, and the wagons began to move forward. Helmut jumped up and took the reins while Arnold and Father walked beside the terrified horse. There was no time for questions. There was no time to complain. There was no time to cry.

The early morning fog swirled over the lake as the wagons lurched forward. It was hard to tell the difference between the cloudy mist and the rising dust from the street. Strangely, as the column moved ahead, the shouting and crying ceased. Nobody spoke as each person took one last look at the abandoned houses and empty yards of Franzfeld. Only the sounds of shuffling hooves and creaking wagons broke the silence.

Holding tightly to the wagon's side, ten-year-old Anita stood and looked back at the only home she had ever known. The door was closed, and she wondered if it would ever be opened again. She could see the small pears on the big tree by the porch and the blooming lilacs along the fence. Anita smiled when she noticed the goats were helping themselves to Mother's vegetable garden. She took one final look at the house. The last thing she saw was the tiny form of her beautiful calico cat. It was sitting at the top of the stairs, watching the line of wagons trail by.

A sharp familiar bark caught her attention. It was Aza, her grandparents' dachshund. She came running from the big gate of their farm, her short legs pumping as fast as they could. Pleased, Anita called to her, hoping someone would put her on the wagon. No one did. Aza followed for a short distance but slowed. She couldn't keep up.

***

Hitler's army moved rapidly, taking city after city. When the Soviets forced the villagers of Franzfeld to leave on that July day, the front line of battle was less than 100 miles away. Suspicious that the Mennonites would collaborate with the invading army because of their German heritage, the Soviets determined that no one could remain behind. Neither would any crops or supplies be left to aid the Germans. It is likely that the evacuees were destined for Siberia or mass execution.

***

The wagon train moved slowly all through the day with just a few breaks to rest the horses. The bumps and jolts amused the children at first, but after a while the constant jarring became irritating. It even seemed hard for Mother. She was still weak from recent childbirth, and the bouncing wagon kept the baby awake and fretful. The baby's crying was constant. There was nothing anyone could do to make things better, and Anita noticed tears on Mother's face, too. She wondered if could be from the smoke that surrounded them.

The fields had all been set on fire, and it was hot—unbearably hot. In every direction, they could see the fires burning. Anita held her hands over her nose as they trudged by one field that burned close to the road. Her little sisters cried, but no one seemed to notice. Her father just marched ahead without a word. Something about the look on his face warned Anita not to speak to him.

At twilight, the wagons stopped near a small creek. The children climbed down, excited to explore the area, but Father insisted they quickly gather sticks for a fire. It was important to hurry because all the children would be looking for wood to give their families, and the supply was limited. Once the wood was gathered, they would have to use dried cow dung, and that wasn't nearly as much fun as racing the other children for sticks.

Helmut and Arnold struggled to start a campfire while Anita's father tended to the horses. The exhausted animals were not used to such a long trek. There were sores and swollen legs to treat. Anita held baby Hansi, who now slept quietly, so her mother could prepare some tea for her tired family. That was the best she could do without food.

Just before dark, someone noticed a tiny figure coming slowly up the road. It was Aza, Grandfather's dog, limping painfully on bleeding paws. Although left behind, she had followed the wagons long after they disappeared. Someone kindly swooped Aza up and brought her to Grandmother, who lay in the wagon. Without a word, Grandmother took the loyal little dachshund in her arms and buried her face in its fur. She knew all too well the soldiers would not allow the dog to stay, and tomorrow Aza would be abandoned again.

They headed ever eastward, away from the battlefront and toward the Dnieper River. There, the Russian army felt it could stop the Germans' advance. The next day brought more pain and misery for people and animals alike. The smoke choked their lungs, their feet blistered, and every bone ached. The sights along the way were gruesome as the swollen bodies of slaughtered livestock littered the roadside, evidence of the Soviets' scorched earth policy.

Hansi no longer cried but lay weakly in his mother's arms. Under such stress and without food, her body could no longer produce milk. Anita watched as her mother, determined to keep her baby alive, took a tiny sugar lump that she had saved, put it in a handkerchief, and dipped it into some water. Placing it in the baby's mouth, she could induce him to suck on the handkerchief. That bit of sugar was just enough.

Relentlessly, the soldiers drove them to hurry along, thinking they would soon reach the river. It did not matter to the soldiers how many might succumb to the pain or hunger. The villagers had to obey orders.

It was late in the afternoon when the wagons were allowed to stop again to water the horses. The men unharnessed and led the horses down to a stream that was lined with trees and thick bushes. Anita and a few others her age decided to explore a nearby field that still had an unburned portion. As they passed through the burned field, they came to a clump of tall stalks containing a strange fruit. They had never seen corn before but gathered some of the ripened ears and returned to the camp. Excited, the adults sent the children right back to gather as much as they could. Within a short time, the entire group was shucking and boiling. Anita was surprised when the adults paused and bowed their heads before eating, giving thanks for the miracle of the unburned field.

The corn was not the only surprise that evening. When the men took the horses down to the water, there were two German soldiers hiding in the bushes. The soldiers told them of the Russian plan to kill their whole group when they reached the Dnieper River bridge. They believed the Russians intended to blow up the bridge with the village wagon train trapped upon it. The German soldiers told them to stall the wagons as much as possible, breaking wheels or harnesses, anything to keep from moving forward. The German army was getting closer, and if the wagon train was overtaken, they would be allowed to return to their village.

The next morning, the villagers were slow getting the horses harnessed, and the Russian guards shouted and threatened. Just after the wagons set out, the wheel on the front wagon spun off, and the wagon lurched sideways, blocking the path. The wheel was repaired several hours later, and the group set off again. Then, another wagon broke down as its horse kicked the wagon tongue and somehow managed to turn the wagon broadside. Close to noon, a harness broke, sending one of the horses running and bucking down the line of wagons. Again, the group halted as the runaway was secured and order was restored. The Russian guards fumed and yelled—but wagon repairs take time.

It was late in the afternoon when Anita heard a strange rumbling noise. It seemed to grow louder by the minute. Curious, she stretched up on her knees and looked toward the rear of the wagon train. At first, she thought just another column of smoke was rising in the distance, but it seemed different this time. Then, she noticed the men and boys outside the wagons gazing rearward as well, and expressions of excitement replaced the looks of fear. She looked around for the Russian guards. She expected to see them waving their rifles and shouting at the men to keep moving. But there were no guards in sight.

Suddenly, the wagons stopped, and Anita heard cheers coming from the men. They waved their hats in the air and clapped each other on the back. Her older brothers jumped excitedly and laughed. She turned to look backwards. A whole company of soldiers was coming up the road, quickly overtaking the wagons. Their weapons were at the ready, expecting resistance from the guards. But the Russian soldiers had fled, and the villagers welcomed them with joy. Anita was confused. She thought the Germans were the enemies of the Soviets—and of her village. Now her parents were cheering the invaders.

The mood in camp that night was much different. The villagers, though extremely weary, were cheerful because the soldiers had shared their supplies with them. That next morning, when they turned their wagons to the west, gratitude and relief filled their hearts. They had been spared the uncertainty of a passage to Siberia or a terrifying death on the bridge over the Dnieper River. Maybe a more hopeful existence awaited them under German control.

During the afternoon, the group paused for a rest near a neighboring Mennonite village. Wanting to stretch their legs, Anita and a few older children ran to explore the area. They entered the village and discovered that it, too, had been evacuated. Spooked by the hushed and deserted atmosphere, the children walked quietly through the town.

Anita noticed a beautiful house with a pretty fence and flower garden. The door was wide open, and it drew the curious children to wonder what a lovely home like this would look like inside. Cautiously, they crept in, afraid that someone might still be there and fuss at them for their bad manners. But all was quiet, the beautiful furniture was clean and tidy, the floor was swept, and the kitchen still smelled of fresh-cut watermelon. Everything remained as if nothing had happened, and the happy family that lived here would arrive home any minute.

Chilled by the eerie silence, the children stood and stared. Not a single hand reached out to touch the pretty dishes, picture books, or the china doll that lay in a toy cradle. Without a word, the children turned and left. Somehow, they knew this family would not be as fortunate as they were.

***

The people in this Mennonite village had made it to the river, and they would not be coming back. By this time, they were on a train bound for the labor camps in Siberia and the far northern areas of the Soviet Union. There, they would join the thousands of other deported Mennonites facing starvation in desperate conditions.

The people of Franzfeld had fallen into the hands of the occupational German forces. Their destiny, although uncertain, was more fortunate than those Russia had managed to evacuate eastward.

For the Mennonites of German heritage, this occupation was welcomed. Free of Soviet control, the village experienced a small cultural revival. Church services were allowed once again, and the school system was reorganized. For a few short seasons, the peaceful Mennonites once again farmed their own land. Far from the battlefront, most were unaware of the horrors their Russian and Jewish neighbors faced throughout Ukraine.

***

Cheers broke out among the villagers as they caught sight of their small village on the horizon. It seemed that hope, after so many difficult and discouraging years, was still alive. Even the exhausted horses seemed to carry their heads a little higher as they neared the safety of their familiar barns.

To their amazement and relief, the village looked exactly as they had left it. Many had feared that the fires would spread and destroy their homes, but they were still there, just as though nothing had happened. As the wagons drew nearer, pets that had been left behind joined in the celebration with a frenzy of yips and tail wagging.

Anita shouted and pointed when she saw her pretty calico cat perched on a fence post. She turned to tell Mother, but her head was bowed, and her lips were moving as if she were talking. Who was she talking to with her eyes shut tight? Anita looked for Father. Surprised, she saw that he had fallen to his knees in the road. His hat was in his hands, and his face was turned upward to the sky.

Chapter 14
German Occupation

It was late in the morning when Anita and her sisters awoke. Exhausted from the wagon trek, they had slept much later than usual in their own beds. There were strange shuffling and thumping noises coming from the living room, and the always nosey Anita dressed quickly and hurried to the kitchen.

There were German soldiers in their house! Curious, she peeked around the corner. Duffle bags, sleeping rolls, cots, and boots occupied almost every corner. It dawned on her that they planned to stay, and by the smile on her mother's face, she determined that her parents had welcomed them. Mother was busy cooking something that smelled wonderful.

"Is that sausage?" Anita brimmed with excitement.

"Yes, the soldiers brought it," her mother smiled. "These men have been assigned to our house, and they offered to share their meat. Look outside, their army food wagon will be staying in our yard, too. We will need to share some of our vegetables in exchange for their German sausage."

Anita hurried outside. There were several soldiers standing around the wagon, and a large kettle was hung over a newly dug firepit. They smiled and spoke to her in German. It was not the Low German that she was used to, but it was familiar enough to understand. Bravely, she greeted them with her best manners. They laughed at her but seemed friendly. They were in good spirits, joking and horsing around, happy to be at ease in a friendly village where they were treated as heroes.

It was all very confusing to Anita. The Red communist soldiers always frowned and shouted at the villagers. Yet, she had been told at school that Germans were the enemies. Why were her parents so pleased? Could she trust these soldiers? She considered these things for a few seconds—but just a few seconds. There was sausage cooking. She waved at the soldiers and ran back to the kitchen.

That evening, Father helped the men set up for another meeting. Where the hammer and sickle flag formerly stood, they hung a different flag with strange black lines. The picture of Stalin was replaced by another—the image of a stern man with a small mustache. The soldiers clicked their heels together and saluted the man, just like the Young Pioneers had been taught to do for Stalin.

Even though Anita was not allowed in the meeting, she could hear everyone cheering. The next morning, she heard the good news. The livestock that previously belonged to the communists had been divided up among the villagers. Each family gained one milk cow, two goats, and a horse. They would also be allowed to plant and harvest the fields for themselves.

It wasn't long before the school was reorganized and opened. New teachers were assigned, and classes began. But this time, no one was permitted to speak Russian. Only German was spoken, and it was not the familiar Plattdeutsch. Each child was to speak and write well in the language of the new leader. They were told that the Führer would be pleased with nothing less. Gone were the days of movies, bonfires, dancers, or magic shows. Anita's teachers were even more strict than before, and she learned a new hand salute. It had to be done perfectly, and at just the right time!

The Mennonite church that had been turned into a theater was once again allowed to be a house of worship, and renovations began. Anita wondered why that building was so special. Why did the villagers take out the big movie screen? Her parents told her that they would be able to worship God now. Who was God? They tried to explain. They said He was the Creator of the universe, powerful and holy, and that He loved righteousness and mercy. Anita listened, but she wasn't sure she could trust what they said. She had always been told that older people did not understand the new ways. Now, her teachers told her that the

Führer knew what was true and that she only needed to obey what he said.

Who was Hitler? Anita had only seen his picture, and he did not look as kind as the grandfatherly Stalin. Yet, she assumed that he was nice because at school she had learned to sing, "What a Friend We Have in Hitler." The teachers said that he was the one who had sent the soldiers to rescue them from the Russians.

When the announcement came that the school was going on a field trip to see Hitler, Anita was very excited. The schoolchildren had never taken a trip to see anything before. It was going to be so much fun, and she couldn't wait to see the famous hero who saved her village. Another famous leader, Mussolini, was supposed to be there also, although she knew little about him.

The next day, the children climbed aboard several horse-drawn buckboards. Rows of rough wooden planks had been nailed in to provide seating for as many children as possible. There was much giggling, laughing, and horseplay as the wagons bumped along the dirt roads. But after a couple of hours, the bumping wasn't quite as fun, and dust filled their noses and choked their throats.

It was August, and as the hot and sweaty children wiped the dirt from their faces, the dusty streaks and smears frustrated the girls in their clean dresses. Of course, it delighted the boys, who loved to make the most of their filthy appearance and threaten the girls with their dirty hands.

Occasionally, the caravan stopped along the way to water the big horses. The children climbed down and stretched, and, if they were quick, splashed some water on their grimy faces.

Finally, the wagons stopped at the intersection of two roads. To Anita's amazement, this road was not dirt; it was hard like a rock. The children stared at the road—none of them had seen pavement before. Some of the boys hopped down from the wagon and tentatively stepped on it. Soon, they were jumping and acting silly. The teachers fussed at them, of course, but before long the whole class was off the wagon and touching the road.

It took a few minutes, but the teachers eventually restored order, and the children were lined up alongside the highway. There they waited, passing the time with simple games and childish chatter. Anita was not one to wait patiently. Several times, she was called out by her teacher for her restless antics.

Suddenly, someone pointed up the road, and all the children paused to listen and look. A vehicle appeared in the distance followed by several others. Anita heard the unfamiliar hum of the engines. She knew these were automobiles, but she had never seen or heard one, and she trembled with anticipation. A bright flash caught her eye as the sun reflected off the shiny metal. She couldn't take her eyes away from the oncoming cars, even when she heard the horse behind her lunging nervously.

The cars came quickly, faster than she could imagine. As they drew closer, the vehicles slowed only slightly. Leaning forward in line, she caught sight of the flags fluttering on either side of the cars and saw the people sitting inside. The roar of the escort vehicles startled her, and she instinctively stepped backward.

"Attention," yelled the teachers. All the students quickly stood upright. "Heil, Hitler!" yelled the teachers. "Heil Hitler!" All the students saluted as the cars drove quickly past. It was over in a moment, and the children spilled out into the road, waving happily at the vanishing cars.

The excitement subsided, and the children obediently climbed back on the wagons for the long trip home. Anita wondered why such an important man would travel on that highway. Why didn't he stop and greet those who cheered him? He didn't even smile. Shouldn't a leader be nice to people who loved him? But these thoughts didn't bother her for very long, and by the time the wagons arrived back in the village, she was slumped against the sideboards and almost asleep.

***

It was on August 28, 1941, that Hitler and Mussolini arrived at the airport of Uman, Ukraine (approximately 150 miles from Franzfeld) to visit the eastern front. They drove to view the German and Italian armies under the command of Field Marshal Gerd von Rundstedt. Hitler's east-

ern Wehrmacht headquarters, called Werwolf, were established just to the east of Uman at Vinnytsya, Ukraine. Hitler would visit this headquarters several times over the course of the next two years of German occupation.

***

Renovations on the church building were completed in the fall. The villagers planned a big ceremony, and the whole town looked forward to the Sunday that followed. Anita was pleased because she thought she might learn more about God. She had asked her parents about it, but they were so busy with new responsibilities that their answers could only be brief and were confusing.

When the day for the ceremony came, the crisp fall weather put everyone in an excited mood. Anita's mother made her a new Sunday dress. It was white with a few bits of lace for decoration. The family gathered in their best clothes on the porch for the short walk to the church.

All the villagers were there, and after a short speech by one of the older men, they all filed in to find their seats. It took a few minutes for the parents to quiet their children, but it was soon understood that there was to be no talking or wiggling during the service. This was not what Anita expected. She had hoped for the exciting atmosphere of the communist school's picture shows. They did sing a song, but it was not one she knew, so she just looked around and exchanged funny faces with the children near her. Then, an old man stood up and read something from a book and made a speech, but the annoyed Anita didn't bother to listen.

With the coming of winter in 1941, services at the church ceased. Not only was it difficult for the villagers to attend, but a new German commander discouraged any public religious activity. News of the Führer's preferences made it clear that all German peoples were to occupy themselves with activities that supported the state. Ukraine, with its rich soil, was expected to help feed the grand army of the Third Reich. Having never participated in "religious activity," Anita did not particularly care, but she was surprised at her parents' disappointment.

On a cold, windy day in January, Anita and her brother, Rudi, made an unexpected discovery. They had accompanied their mother as she attended to their invalid grandmother's needs. The twins were left alone in Grandfather's parlor to wait quietly. It was usually boring, but on this day, they found a great book lying on a table. They had never seen a book like it before. In fact, there were very few books in their village except in the school, so this was an opportunity that couldn't be missed. With some effort, they carried the heavy book to the couch, sat down, and carefully examined it.

It was bound with intricately stamped leather covers that felt like wood. A metal clasp held it closed, but nimble fingers managed to snap it open. The pages were printed with German lettering, but the ornate style made the words difficult to read. To the twins' delight, there were more than words in this book. As they turned the pages of the beautiful hardcover, it opened to a picture of a man and a woman walking in a garden. Another page showed a large line of people walking next to a giant wall of water. Fascinated, they turned to other engravings. Anita sensed that each picture told a story, but she had never heard any of these.

One picture particularly attracted her, and she stared at every detail trying to understand the story it told. In it, there were many people crying and lying on the ground. Suddenly she realized that they were all surrounded by big snakes wrapping around their bodies and biting them. Some people were reaching out for help, and others were dying from the snakebites. What kind of snakes were these? The snakes in her life, in the cellar and the ones her brothers caught, weren't dangerous. She assumed that the snakes in the picture were poisonous and deadly.

Anita shuddered as she imagined big snakes slithering around her ankles. Searching the picture again, she noticed an old man holding up a large stick with another snake coiled around it. As she studied the drawing, she observed that the people on the ground were reaching toward the man with the stick. No matter how hard she tried, Anita could not figure out the story before her. What could it all mean?

Just then, their mother came in and gasped when she saw what her children were doing. Carefully, she lifted the big book and took it to the corner of the room.

"Mother, what is that book, and why have we never seen it?" Rudi stared up at Mother.

"It is a Bible, and you must promise me that you will not mention that you have seen it," said Mother. "That book is very important to your Grandfather, and if the soldiers knew, they might steal it."

"A Bible!" said Anita. "They told us in school that we should never read one. Its words are dangerous!"

Mother's face darkened with anger. "They told you a lie, Anita." And under her breath, "Their words are poison."

***

Katharina knew how precious the Bible was to her father and how carefully he guarded it for many years. It had been hidden from the authorities, and only now with the Germans in control had he dared to bring it out. Yet, Katharina worried because she had heard that the new German commander disapproved of religious books. She feared the consequences if the soldiers knew what the children had discovered. Anita did not know all this, of course, nor was she aware that her parents prayed for her daily. Through the pages of her grandfather's Bible, a tiny seed had been planted in her heart.

Chapter 15
Cold Hearts—1942

Winter was difficult for the German soldiers stationed in the village. It was much colder than their homeland, and they grew sullen and restless. Anita learned to stay out of their way, especially the lieutenant. He was meaner than the others.

Although the villagers had more freedom, the regulations under German rule were difficult to understand. Many were required to change their names. Uncle Abraham, Anita was instructed, would be addressed as Uncle Henry.

Occasionally, Anita heard rumors of Ukrainians who were forced to work or fight in the army while older girls were sent away to serve as maids. She also heard stories of towns where many had been executed by the Germans. For some reason, her Jewish neighbors were required to wear badges with a star on them, and there were always rumors of spies or informants.

The Germans even thought that two of Anita's childhood friends were spies. They had been taken by the Soviet communists the year before. When they escaped and returned to the village, the Germans captured them and accused them of being Russian spies. Fortunately, because the boys spoke both German and Russian, they were used as translators and not executed.

Sadly, Anna, the hired servant of Brumm Bear and a special friend to Anita, did not have the same fate. She was walking across the muddy wagon road when a military vehicle came barreling down the street. The soldiers were honking the horn and laughing, hollering at her to get out of the road. Unfortunately, the loud noises brought on one of

Anna's seizures. She stiffened and contorted. She flailed about, striking at unseen tormentors. With no effort to avoid her, the vehicle struck her and crushed her beneath its tires. The soldiers stopped for a moment, only to laugh and drive away.

No one dared question the authority of the soldiers. So, the people did not complain. They were too afraid.

Chapter 16
Flight to Germany—1943

It was late August when rumors began to swirl that caused great concern. The Soviet army was retaking Ukrainian territory, and the Germans were retreating. Her parents told her nothing, but Anita noticed the worried frown that never left her father's face. What would happen if the Soviets came back? Her family kept German soldiers in their home, and that would make the Russians angry. Would her father disappear like so many others? It was easy when she was younger to ignore the worried looks, but she was twelve now, and fearful thoughts began to trouble her.

That night, there was another meeting in their house. The big picture of Hitler was placed carefully, and the swastika flag hung on the wall. When the village men gathered, the stern German commander marched in without a word or even a polite nod to Mother as she opened the door.

"Heil Hitler." His boots clapped together.

"Heil Hitler," the villagers answered.

The commander paced as he spoke with his back straight and his hands clasped behind his back. "Tomorrow, you will make preparations to evacuate this village. You are ordered to proceed to Poland where you will be processed and registered as citizens of Greater Germany. We will depart the day after tomorrow. Pack only what you can carry in one bag. You will travel by wagon to Vinnytsya. You will then board the train for Litzmannstadt. There, your wagons, draft horses, and any excess possessions will be taken for military purposes. These are the Führer's orders. There will be no exceptions. Dismissed."

Not one word was spoken as the commander snapped his heels, turned, and walked out. Then, chaos erupted as the overwhelmed men clamored with groans, shouts, and weeping. Slowly, they filed out with hanging heads and slumped shoulders. They would have to return home, inform their families, and prepare for what lay ahead.

With her ear pressed to the wall, Anita heard what the commander said. She did not understand all of it, but she sensed that something terrible was about to happen. Her stomach churned as she imagined another wagon trek. Would they come back home this time? Her head spun as Father shouted. It was time for the family to join him in the kitchen.

"Children," Father began. "Our leaders have told us that we must move to another town. You will not be able to take any of your toys or extra clothes. We have only one day to prepare enough food for several days. We don't know how long. I will rely on each of you to help. Arnold, I will need you to help me kill and dress a goat that we will cook tomorrow. Helmut, I want you and Rudi to catch two rabbits from the pit to slaughter. Anita, you must help your mother make bread tonight. Lene, you must do your best to take care of Katie and Hansi."

There was no time for questions. There was no time to complain. There was no time to cry. There was just a flurry of activity as the family desperately tried to prepare for the journey.

Anita worked until late in the night. Exhausted, she fell into bed for a few hours of sleep, then woke very early to begin again. She hardly knew what she was doing. There was so much noise. Villagers hustled back and forth, animals ran about wildly, wagons rattled by, and Hansi and her little sisters would not stop crying.

Father and her brothers slaughtered animals and prepared meat, although it was uncertain whether the provisions would last in the hot summer sun. They did not know the length of the journey, but it was definite that no food would be available to buy along the way. Sausages, bread, pickled eggs, and dried fruit needed to be packaged carefully for the family to survive the long trek.

Frantically, they worked through the night. Once, Anita stopped and listened. She heard booming in the distance. A high-pitched yell from her mother brought her attention back. Anita ran to the garden, gathering what vegetables were available. Lene helped dig the small, unripe potatoes, and together they filled a basket.

As soon as dawn broke, the boys worked to harness their horse, wild-eyed from the surrounding chaos. All around, wagons bumped along, pulled by nervous animals that half-trotted, half-plunged up the road.

"Where is the baby?" Mother screamed.

"I have him," Rudi answered. "Helmut has Katie."

Climbing and scrambling, the children tumbled into the wagon. Anita found a spot and looked over the sides of the wagon. In every direction, she saw people yelling and running. All the village cows, pigs, and goats had been turned loose to fend for themselves, and the dogs were in a frenzy as they chased them back and forth. Barn doors were thrown wide, fence gates swung free, and the shutters and houses stood open.

"Father," Anita cried in a panic as she looked through their kitchen window. "We left the lantern lit in the house."

"It's too late, now," he answered. Without even a glance, he slapped the reins on the horse's back, and the wagon jolted forward.

Gripping tight to the lurching wagon, Anita looked back. Would they return like they did last time? She watched home grow smaller and smaller as they headed west. Beyond the village, toward the horizon, she saw tiny light flashes and drifting smoke. She counted three seconds between the booming guns.

Soon the horse settled into a trot, and the wagon rolled along steadily. Exhausted, Anita lay down on the blankets that Mother had put in the wagon bed. Within minutes, she was asleep.

Chapter 17
The Trek

With a jolt, Anita woke up. When she opened her eyes, a dark sky loomed above. Only a few faint stars winked between the drifting clouds. It took a moment, but then she remembered where she was and looked to find her parents. Her father was hunched at the front with the reins wrapped around his elbow. His head drooped forward. She thought he might be asleep. Her mother sat with her back against the bench seat, but she, too, seemed to be asleep. Hansi was huddled at her side, and Katie's head lay in her lap.

Rudi stirred nearby. "Oh, you are awake. I thought you might be dead."

"Where are Helmut and Arnold?" Anita asked sleepily.

"Walking, helping the horse." Rudi got to his knees and began to climb out.

"Where are you going?" Anita whispered, not wanting to wake the others.

"It's my turn to walk," Rudi answered softly. "I think we plan to stop and let the horse rest, but Arnold will want to keep going soon. Father needs rest, too. He has been awake for two days."

"Two days!" Anita couldn't believe it. "Have I been asleep for two days?

She tried to get to her knees, but her head hurt, and the rocking wagon made her lose balance.

"Lie down, Anita," her mother whispered. "You have been sick. You can get up when we stop."

Slowly, Anita lay back down. Her stomach churned, and the clouds swirled above her. Closing her eyes, she soon fell asleep again.

Several days passed. Anita did not know how many. Sometimes she walked, sometimes she slept, but she was always tired. It was hard to be cheerful and not complain. Her fever had passed, but she was still weak. She had little appetite, which was good because they needed to be sparing with the food they had.

They were not far from Vinnytsya, but the wagon train moved slowly because the animals were exhausted. Soon, she heard they were close to reaching the train station. She clasped her hands together in eager expectation, filled with curiosity.

Before long, she could see the city. Strange noises she had never heard grew louder. The air smelled smoky, and a sudden whistle split the air as a huge train engine came out of nowhere. She realized that the train tracks were to the left, and a long line of train cars came into view.

Suddenly, a staccato burst of gunfire made her scream and cover her ears tightly. Everyone around her dropped to the ground or dove behind the wagons. A plane roared overhead and climbed higher in the sky. Another plane screamed by and banked sharply to the right.

Looking up, Anita saw four, maybe five planes all flying in different directions. Two seemed to be racing, but then gunfire rattled, and one plane burst into flames.

The German soldiers shouted at everyone to hurry up. Exhausted horses were whipped, and the whole column moved faster and faster toward the train station. The planes flew away, but the soldiers yelled even more and directed the wagons to a stopping place.

"Move, move! Get to the dock! Leave your wagons. Take only your pack—nothing more." The soldiers bellowed. "Women and children to the dock, immediately."

Anita held Katie's hand as she ran to her mother. Her mother, holding Hansi, grabbed Lene's hand and pushed Anita in front of her. Together, they hurried to the loading dock. Anita looked back at her brothers and Father. Were they coming?

The planes had returned, their engines roaring above them. All around her, people were running and screaming. The train whistled again, the guns rattled, and the sound of hundreds of boots on the wooden dock rumbled like an earthquake.

"Don't let go of Katie, Anita. Stay close," Mother shouted.

A line of cattle cars pulled up close to the dock. The soldiers scrambled over the side and yanked open the big door of the train car.

"Quickly, get inside," commanded the soldiers. "Keep moving, all the way to the back."

The women and children clambered into the stock car. More and more were driven in. Anita was pushed deep into the car. More came on. Somehow, Mother had managed to get them all to the back corner. They huddled together, standing. There was not enough room to sit down.

Strangely, it was quiet inside the boxcar. Even the youngest had been shocked into silence. No whining, no weeping, only the sounds of shuffling as the exhausted refugees accepted the conditions without protest.

The train began to move. The train whistle screamed again, piercing the noiseless stock car. It lurched forward and stopped again and again as another boxcar pulled into position at the dock. Finally, the train picked up speed. The mechanical jostling of the wheels soothed the babies, and their mothers began to relax.

From her position in the corner, Anita took a moment to look around. The stock car was made of wood with one small window on each side. The wooden slats were close together, but she found a crack between two boards where she could see out if she put her eye right up against it. Fortunately, the small hole to the outside also offered a little fresh air. With so many people standing tightly together, the stale air inside was not very pleasant.

The little children around her sank to the floor by their mothers' feet. There was straw scattered about, but it was not enough to cushion them against the bumps and jolts as the train rumbled on. The older girls and the adults had to stand. Anita looked around at some of the women. She knew most of them, but they were hard to recognize. Some familiar faces were streaked with tears, others so worn-looking that she could barely identify them. Worried expressions were everywhere, but the ones that made her stare were those with bowed heads and lips silently moving.

Hours later, Anita woke with a start. She had been given a turn to sit on the floor and had fallen into a restless sleep. By huddling closer together, the group had made enough space for some of the children and elderly to sit down for a short rest.

Anita stood up and moved to the side where she could peek between the wooden slats. They were moving through a forest. The trees glistened from fresh rain, and the air was clean and crisp. The leaves were just beginning to turn, and Anita imagined what it would be like to explore those inviting woods.

Suddenly, the train began to slow.

"Get ready to jump, Anita," her mother called. "We can get off for just a few minutes and run into the forest for relief." She paused. "But don't take long; they won't wait for you."

Yes, Anita needed a break. From the crammed corner, she moved her way through legs and limbs to reach the big door. Someone slid it open, and the passengers jumped and climbed down from the train. The train did not stop but moved at a very slow crawl.

She ran the short distance to the woods and quickly found a protected spot and squatted. The train kept moving. Hurriedly, she finished and headed back to the tracks. Anita ran along the side of the train until she heard her mother calling to her at the right boxcar. Beyond and all around, children were shouting and racing, searching for their family's car. They scrambled and stumbled as they tried to get back on the train. For Anita, a hand extended. She took hold and climbed aboard.

Holding onto the side of the door, Anita looked back at the woods and watched children still trying to swing aboard as the train picked up speed. Such a commotion! Some older children, like her, were laughing and giggling. Mothers were out of breath and counting heads to see if everyone made it back.

Suddenly, Anita noticed a small figure on one side of the woods. It was her cousin, Katie. She came out of the trees close to the end of the train. To Anita's horror, Katie stumbled and fell.

"Mother," Anita yelled. "Katie is still back there!" Everyone in the boxcar craned to look. They called out for Katie to run faster. They screamed at the soldier to stop the train. He laughed and shook his head.

Anita watched from the side as the train moved farther and farther away, and the little figure got smaller and smaller. She saw Katie fall again. This time, she did not get up. Anita's eyes filled with tears. She turned to see Katie's mother weeping, collapsed on the floor. Other women held her tightly, trying to comfort her.

"What will happen to Katie?" Anita asked her mother.

"We can only hope that other trains will come after us, and they will see her," her mother said quietly. "Someone from the village will see her and know her and bring her with them." Somehow, she didn't sound very hopeful. Tears welled in her eyes.

Chapter 18
Litzmannstadt

It was early morning when the train pulled into the station at Litzmannstadt, Germany. The tired and hungry refugees filed out, wearily following the group into a large room where instructions were being given. Anita was too far away to hear what the soldier said and too exhausted to care. She just walked along with the rest as they moved from place to place.

"Take off your clothes, Anita," her mother said as she undressed her sisters.

Startled, Anita burst out, "Why? I don't want to."

"You must. We are to be deloused."

"What's a louse?" Anita pulled away, and her mother sighed, stepping back and putting her hands on her hips.

"Hush, child. It's an insect, and we must do what they say. Now, quickly take off your clothes and put them in that bin."

"I don't have any bugs, and I won't take off my clothes." Anita wouldn't budge.

But her protests were useless. Soldiers surrounded the refugees, and a big German woman stood nearby to see that every refugee complied. She took a step forward, and fear ran down Anita's spine. Fuming, Anita took off her clothes and put them in the bin, looking around to see if any boys could see her. No, there were just hundreds of women, girls, and small children, all naked.

They were ushered into a large room. It had a low ceiling, and there were metal pipes with little holes in them sticking out about every three feet. The floor was covered with tiles that reminded her of the much prettier floors in her school at Nikolaifeld.

Suddenly, a loud sound made all the women look up at the ceiling—just in time to receive a blast of water from the showerheads. Screams and cries filled the large room as cold water shocked their skin. The shouts halted all at once. Mouths filled with foul-tasting water. The taste was sharp and overwhelming—it was bug poison.

Fortunately, it was over soon. The women and girls filed out, soaked and shivering. They were sent to tables where clothing was stacked high. Each was handed various items that might or might not fit. Even so, they were thankful to have them.

The next hours were spent waiting, sitting, standing, or moving from one room to the next. Anita was relieved when she spotted her father and brothers. They registered their names and occupations, education, and family history, answering hundreds of questions and undergoing physical examinations.

Hours later, they boarded another train to reach their assigned refugee camp. An overnight train ride and a short drive in the back of a big truck brought them to a cluster of large, white, two-story buildings. The place was plain, without charm. This was their temporary home until arrangements could be made for housing.

Chapter 19
Hindenburg

The most significant detail about Anita's new home was a large metal fence. It stood eight feet tall, topped with rows of sharp barbed wire. The gate was shut tight and guarded by armed soldiers. It was not like the low fence back at the village. That fence prevented animals from escaping onto the wagon road. This one kept people inside.

The buildings were two and three stories tall with many big rooms. Her family was assigned an area in a large room on the third floor. There were several other families settling in nearby. They would be sleeping on the floor because there were no beds or furniture. No matter, they had no possessions to put away in closets.

Somewhere downstairs was a big kitchen. The women organized a cooking schedule and took turns providing meals for the families in each room. Minimal supplies of flour and other essentials were provided. That was good news because the food supplies they had brought with them were gone, and Anita longed for just about anything to fill her stomach.

Their room had windows overlooking an alley. Anita was pleased that she could look out and see houses and a city street with shops nearby. These were new sights for her, and she took in every detail.

As she stared, she saw a bright spot of blue in the house that was closest to her window, just across the alley. Surprisingly, the spot moved, and the window opened. Anita realized it was a young girl in a bright blue dress. Anita waved at her. The girl waved back. Anita smiled and waved enthusiastically.

From the front window of the building, she watched the activities on the wide road that ran past the camp. A few days later, she watched as groups of prisoners marched up the road, escorted by several armed guards and big dogs. One group looked proud and wore uniforms. "British prisoners," explained Mother. Another group was ragged and stumbled as they moved slowly down the road. "Russian prisoners," she heard Father say. She could tell that the Russian soldiers were starving because when a wagon dropped potatoes, they picked them up and ate them raw.

It did not take long for the family to settle into a difficult but monotonous routine. Father and Arnold were assigned to work in the coal mine nearby. They would leave early in the morning and arrive back late in the evening, exhausted and covered in dust. Mother worked endlessly to provide meals and maintain a semblance of cleanliness for her young family confined in such a small area. Cooking, washing, mending, and all other familiar tasks were much harder than before. None of the tools for these chores were easily available, and "making do" was the new norm.

It was necessary for Anita to tend to her little sisters and brothers. They discovered that they were allowed to roam the compound and play outdoors, but this would soon end with the coming of winter.

Anita began each day at the window to wait for the girl next door to come and wave to her. Even though they could not speak, Anita felt sure that they were friends.

One morning, the young girl waved vigorously and kept motioning toward the fence. Curious, Anita went down the stairs and out the front door. Then, she saw her new friend coming across the open space between the houses and the tall fence. The girl's mother accompanied her, and they carried a package. As they both came to the fence, the neighbor shyly did not say much, but she took the package and shoved it under the fence. Anita pulled it through and opened it up. Inside were two dresses of beautiful soft colors and fine cloth.

Speechless, she turned to her friend.

"Quickly, child," her friend's mother called. "We must go before the guards come."

"Thank you!" Anita called out and scampered back into the building. She wished she could have talked to her and at least found out her name, but the refugees were not permitted to talk with people outside the fence. She hugged the package and wished with all her might that her friend could understand how much this meant. Why did she do such a kind thing? Maybe she knew that Anita and her family had no other clothes. Anita determined to wear one of the dresses the next day when she waved to her neighbor. Maybe the girl would be able to see how thankful she was if she twirled around in front of the window.

Racing upstairs, she quickly ducked behind a blanket that her mother had hung for privacy and slipped into the dress. It was beautiful. And it fit! She had never owned such a wonderful dress. To her surprise, the dress had a pocket, and tucked inside of a little white handkerchief were four small coins. Thrilled, she ran to the window and, just as she hoped, there was her friend. Anita waved happily and twirled and twirled and twirled.

Anita had never received money before and had no idea what to do with it. What could she buy in this place? Her twin brother, Rudi, came up with a great idea. Helmut, Rudi, and a few other boys had secretly dug a hole under the fence at night. They planned to sneak out and go into the town, and if she was quiet, they'd let her go with them.

The next day, the teens emerged one by one under the fence and ran for cover in the nearby alley. Then, they casually walked down the sidewalk to the shops. All along the street stood vendor carts, and some of the stores had a display outside. Fascinated, Anita examined each one she passed. One cart held fruit from local farmers. The apples were gigantic and red, unlike the crab apples she was familiar with. She withheld herself and did not touch a single thing.

The shopkeepers eyed the teenagers sharply, but they pretended not to notice. Anita took her time and looked with wonder at all the amazing items for sale. She wanted to buy something with her coins. She took them out so the shopkeepers would know that she was not going to take something without paying for it. One noticed and kindly pointed to a display of postcards. They had pictures of beautiful girls with fancy dresses. They would be easy to carry and keep hidden, so Anita decided to buy a few. She asked the shopkeeper how many cards she could buy with her few coins. He told her, and she carefully picked out ten of the most beautiful cards on the rack. This would be her treasure to keep forever.

Postcards from Hindenburg

The boys were anxious to head back before they got caught, so the teens turned around and retraced their steps to the camp. One by one they ducked under the fence, keeping careful watch for the patrolling guards.

It was only a few days later when an announcement was made that all children ages twelve and up were to immediately report to the front of the building. She, Rudi, and Helmut ran downstairs. Anita hoped they would get new clothes, candy, or maybe some books from a library.

Instead, without any explanation, they were instructed to board buses—boys on one, girls on another. The teens soon realized that they were being taken from the camp. Some protested, others cried, but the adults in charge gave no answers. There was no chance to say goodbye to their families.

Anita was a little frightened, but she had learned in the village school that Germany wanted all young people to help their country and be trained to serve Hitler. That was fine with her. Anything was better than staying locked up in the camp and taking care of her little sisters all day. She was thirteen, big enough to do something important. Besides, her parents didn't really understand how meaningful it was to work for the state.

"Silence, girls," shouted a stern woman at the front of the bus. "You are all to be Hitler's children now. You must do exactly as you are told."

A girl sniffled. The woman glared at her. "No crying. The girls of Germany do not cry." Slowly, she walked up the aisle of the bus looking each girl in the face, measuring their worth.

Anita felt mesmerized by the steely face and unblinking eyes of the woman. The staunch woman held her head upright and craned her neck as she studied each refugee. The bus swayed in the traffic, but the woman's head stayed in one spot as her body followed the vehicle's movement. It reminded Anita of the little snakes from the lake that held their heads still while their bodies slithered. It was almost funny, but Anita did not giggle—she would not dare. This snake just might bite.

Hours later, the bus arrived at a big white building. The girls filed out and entered quietly. There, they were handed a small cluster of uniform clothes and assigned a room number. Each was also given a haircut.

The girls were informed that they were now part of the *Bund Deutscher Mädel*, the League of German Girls in the Hitler Youth. Like all German girls, they were to be trained for leadership in the new German society and schooled in manners, academics, homemaking, and physical fitness under the strictest guidelines. This was designed to prepare them for their adult roles in German society: wife, mother, and homemaker. The building was meant to be their home until they turned eighteen.

Chapter 20
League of German Girls

Most days started and ended the same. Early each morning, leaders awoke the girls and hurried them down to the basement where they stripped to the waist and washed with icy cold water. This exercise naturally involved much screaming and laughing.

Quickly drying, they marched back to their dorm rooms to dress in a crisp white shirt, black skirt, and black tie. Each bed had to be made perfectly and everything put away neatly. Then, the girls took their place in line while the leader inspected their beds. If the blanket was not perfectly smooth, she yanked it from the bed and threw it on the floor to be redone.

Anita

Completely silent, the girls marched to the dining hall, which held long tables with ten chairs and an assigned position for each girl. The girls stood behind their seats while the leader instructed them to give thanks to Adolf Hitler for the bread he provided. At the command, they quietly took their seats, sitting up straight with both hands positioned by their plates. They sat and waited at attention until the director picked up her knife and fork. Immediately after breakfast, the girls marched back up to their rooms to collect their schoolbooks—and redo their beds, if necessary. Then, they returned downstairs to fall in line for the march to the nearby classrooms. An exercise routine of calisthenics prepared them for the long hours of schoolwork.

At lunch, the girls were given a piece of bread with jam. Then, it was back to the classroom and more schoolwork. The girls participated in physical education in the afternoon where they ran drills, races, and learned various track and field skills.

Once these activities were finished, it was time to march back to the dormitory and prepare for dinner, where they again silently took their seats at the tables. At this meal, the director often asked them to sing "What a Friend We Have in Hitler." The song made them feel like all the tireless rigor was a privilege because they were serving Hitler and the German state. They were reminded that the Führer provided everything they had.

After dinner, the schoolbooks were brought to the tables in the dining room for study hall. There was always homework to be done in the evening, and absolutely no talking was allowed. Two hours dragged by until the girls were told to march upstairs and prepare for bed.

No one was permitted to speak or make noise after the lights went out. That was fine by Anita because, like the other girls, she was exhausted. Besides, the next day would come quickly with the same rigorous schedule.

For Anita, this new life was exciting. She enjoyed being away from the boredom of housework and babysitting. Anita especially looked forward to the weekends, when the girls marched to a nearby wooded park and were allowed to play games, chasing each other and hiding in the woods.

Sometimes, the girls saw the boys from the Hitler Youth marching nearby. Although they were never permitted to speak to them, there was much giggling and pointing and waving. Occasionally, one of the boys glanced in their direction and, of course, was sharply reprimanded.

On one formal occasion, the boys paraded by with flags flying. The girls were instructed to stand and salute when they passed. As the color guard drew near, Hitler's bold flag fluttered. The lines of the swastika wiggled and writhed. Looking up at the flag, Anita's attention suddenly flashed back to a scene she recalled from Grandfather's book.

Snakes, Anita thought. *It looks like snakes.* Mesmerized, she stared. She remembered the picture with the people dying from their bites.

"Anita!" hissed the director. "Attention!"

Immediately, Anita stiffened, threw her arm up, and shouted, "Heil Hitler!" to the snakes as they slithered their way down the street.

Months passed, and the schedule never changed. Yet Anita was content. After so much uncertainty and fear as a refugee, her routine seemed safe and sure. She felt proud to be a part of the group and was determined to serve Hitler well.

"Räder müssen rollen für den Sieg. Kinderwagen für die nächste krieg. Wheels must roll for victory! Baby buggies for the next war!" This was a slogan that the girls memorized.

Anita did not reminisce about her family very often. She was too busy, and the girls were taught to remember their purpose as Hitler Youth and hide emotional weakness. Only once at Christmas was her mother allowed to visit, and that was for just a few hours.

For this reason, it came as a shock when the girls learned they would be sent back to their families. They were told that the state needed them to help with the war effort in their communities. It was 1945, and Germany was losing the war. Money for the youth programs was no longer available.

Chapter 21
Eichholz—1945

The Friesens had been transferred to Eichholz, a small farming village east of Münster. Germans were ordered to take in refugees, so a farm building designed for grain storage was the family's new home. They were all required to work in the fields while Anita's father was assigned to the local carpentry shop.

Home was different now. The war changed things. For one, Arnold had been shot and was in the hospital. While walking down a road toward the village, a British pilot spotted him and followed him down the lane. Arnold managed to dodge the first pass, but the pilot turned back and made another run at him. The second round of bullets whizzed by and only just missed. Arnold stumbled, fell, and lay still, pretending to be dead. But the pilot turned again for a third pass. This time a bullet hit his foot. Arnold escaped with his life, but from then on, he nursed a furious hatred for the British. But Anita knew that secretly, her parents were grateful. Although his injury was serious and required a long rehabilitation, their eldest was spared the horrors of the battlefront.

Helmut

Helmut was not so fortunate. Not long after Anita arrived at her new home, German soldiers came to their house and demanded that Helmut go with them. At age sixteen, Helmut was taken to help the German army with the "last ditch defense." Germany was determined to fight to the last man, and that included teenagers. Rudi, fifteen, was miraculously spared, although many Hitler Youth of his age were drafted.

For Anita, life at Eichholz was full of challenges. The family lived in a small apartment below a granary. Her mother was forced to bake bread for the farm workers, yet she was only allowed to keep a small portion. They were given war rations, but there was never enough to feed the family.

Anita and Rudi went to school in the morning, but the afternoon was occupied with work in the garden. Long hours of weeding and digging kept them tired and always hungry.

Anita

In all that her family faced, Anita was determined to help provide for her little sisters and embarked on a temporary life of crime. Sometimes at night she sneaked into the farm's forbidden orchard and stole whatever fruit she could find. When no one was looking, she climbed to the grain storage area, filled a bag with wheat kernels, and slipped off to the mill to have them ground into flour.

The owner of the farm was a very wealthy baroness. She hated putting up with the refugees, and she did not provide any kind of help to the family—or anyone else. Even when starving German soldiers came begging, she refused. Anita's mother, on the other hand, always shared a little borsch soup with the hungry men. The baroness' rules were strictly enforced, and Anita's theft would have been punished severely if discovered. But the resourceful teen managed to conceal her evening heists, and her mother's unspoken gratitude for the contraband was worth the risk.

Chapter 22
Winter in Nordwalde

As the air turned crisp and cold, Anita's family was transferred to Nordwalde, a larger town in the north. It was lovely, surrounded by forests and mountains. Once again, Anita and her siblings attended school in the morning but were required to work in the afternoon. This time, she was assigned to a textile factory.

Because of its northern location, Nordwalde hadn't suffered much damage from the bombings. Still, air raid sirens often sounded. There were a variety of signals. Long alarms alerted of a possible attack. Short and loud ones meant that attack was imminent and everyone needed to take shelter.

Occasionally during the winter they had time for play, although the dangers of war were always present. One snowy day, the local children and teens were out sledding on a nearby hill. It was a joyful, light-hearted day—at first.

The children did not realize the significance of their location. The hill they played on descended right down to the edge of an airfield, a possible target for Allied planes.

Suddenly, above the noise of children laughing, the drone of planes buzzed like a thousand wasps. Too late, the children realized that the war planes were coming right toward them. Mothers watching at the top of the hill screamed in terror and came racing for their children.

Bullets slapped the snow all around as the pilots unleashed their firepower, determined to damage the runway. The children, recognizing the danger, dove into the bordering ravines. Sleds flew and bounced as the terrified children tumbled into cover.

One after another, the fighter planes roared overhead, drowning out the noise of the screaming children and the shrieks of mothers sprinting toward their little ones. By the time it was over, they were all trembling and thoroughly shaken. Miraculously, none of the children were seriously injured, and together they hurried home. The teenagers, of course, found the whole thing amusing, telling and retelling the grand story of their daring escape.

The battle, however, was not over. Most of the German planes were destroyed, but a few made it off the tarmac, and a dogfight ensued. Anita watched, mesmerized, as the fighters zoomed back and forth, spitting bullets and smoke. One British plane caught fire and spiraled down.

A few hours later, Mother asked her to go into town for some supplies. She hopped on one of the few trolleys heading her direction and was surprised to see soldiers there as well—two wounded British pilots. The prisoners were sitting on the floor and bleeding profusely. One of them had dark hair and kind eyes. He was looking at her. Their eyes met for a long moment. She felt his discouragement, his weakness. Her heart welled with sympathy. This might be the enemy, but he needed help, and Anita wished she could help him escape. Right then, she determined that one day, she would be someone who helped suffering people.

Often, when the Allied planes stopped bombing, Rudi and Anita were sent to the village to buy food with their ration coupons. Long lines awaited them, and usually almost no food was available. The teenagers were frequently delayed when air raid sirens blasted, sending them to take refuge in a bomb shelter. So, Anita started planning ahead, bringing a book to read for the long hours of waiting.

One day after standing in a long line, Anita scored some cornbread and a little horsemeat. But walking home, the sirens blared again. Foolishly, she decided to run home because she didn't want to spend all day in the bomb shelter. Planes thundered overhead, artillery firing and bombs falling. Anita dove for the safety of a ditch, landing hard on her package and crushing the precious cornbread into tiny crumbs. Terrified, she looked back and saw buildings collapsing, bricks and rubble flying, and people running for their lives. A whistling sound shrieked, and, at the sound of impact, the wall next to her began to crumble. Breathlessly, she grabbed her package and ran as fast as she could toward home.

She nearly tripped over her mother and little sisters when she burst into the room. They were huddled on the floor on their knees praying for her and Rudi, who, wisely, was sitting in the bomb shelter. Proudly, Anita shrugged her shoulders and handed her mother what she had risked her life for—a bag of cornbread crumbs and horsemeat.

Chapter 23
The War Ends

It was early May 1945. Rudi and Anita set off for another day at school. When they arrived, they spied the headmaster standing outside the door of the building. The twins snapped to attention and saluted.

"Heil Hitler!" Anita shouted. Rudi was less enthusiastic—he hated saluting.

"*Guten Tag*," the headmaster replied. "There is no school today. You may go home."

Surprised, the twins stopped short. This was very unusual. He always demanded and returned the Nazi salute. It was very strange, but they didn't dwell on it too long. It would be nice to have a free morning. They headed home.

"No school?" their mother said. "Well, head to town and see if you can buy some food."

The trolley wasn't running, so they had to walk the whole way. When they arrived, the town looked deserted. There were no stores open, no people about, and no traffic of any kind. They came to a bridge and looked for an open store but stopped in their tracks. In front of them was a long silver cylinder embedded in the concrete.

"It's a bomb," whispered Rudi. "Don't go near it. It might explode." For once, Anita kept her mouth shut and did as Rudi said. The bomb was about five feet long and directly in their path. They backed away and retraced their steps. Tension in the air and a sense of disquiet gripped them; the town was so empty.

They returned home, this time following a path by the railroad tracks. Suddenly, a whistle shrieked, and they heard a train approaching. It was coming slowly, and it was full of shouting, happy soldiers leaning out of the windows and waving their caps. They were British soldiers! As they passed, the soldiers threw candy and gum from the windows. People began coming out of the nearby houses, and children ran to gather the candy. Rudi and Anita joined in.

"War is over!" one of the soldiers yelled in broken German.

"Does that mean Germany has been defeated?" asked Rudi quietly. "What will happen now?"

Anita did not know. Should she be happy or sad? Maybe now it would be easier to find food. Maybe they would go back to Franzfeld. At least there would be no more bombing, and maybe Helmut could come home. She waved back to one of the British soldiers.

Later that day, British soldiers came down the street and approached their house.

"Quickly, girls, hide in the loft," whispered her mother as she frantically hurried the girls and glanced about for anything that might incriminate her family. "Rudi, sit down and pretend to be reading."

Three soldiers knocked, and they were let inside. None of them spoke German. They looked around the room and opened the side doors. They talked to Rudi and wrote some notations in a book. A friendly Black soldier spoke to three-year-old Hansi and offered to shake his hand. Hansi drew back, afraid. He had never seen a Black man before.

They left without a word and continued down the street to the next house.

"What did they want, Mother?" asked Anita, climbing out of her hiding place.

"I don't know. There are rumors that those who came from Ukraine will be sent back to Russia. We may not be welcome here. The Germans don't want us now."

Anita knew that was true. The Russian children taunted them because they spoke German. Here the German teenagers insulted them because they were Russian. The authorities declared that they were "stateless" refugees. What were Mennonites anyway? Were they like the gypsies, who had no place to call home?

***

The Yalta Conference in February 1945, which included Franklin D. Roosevelt, Winston Churchill, and Joseph Stalin, established a provision that required the repatriation of all Soviet citizens to the USSR. This provision applied to ethnic Germans who had fled into Germany. Hundreds of thousands were sent back, not to Ukraine but to Siberia and into forced labor camps. At the end of the war, those lucky enough to have ended up in the British- and American-occupied territories had a slim chance of requesting protection from the aggressive tactics of Bolshevik agents. They had the opportunity to immigrate to another country.

The Mennonite Central Committee was an organization dedicated to rescuing displaced Mennonites and establishing colonies in countries such as Canada, the United States, and South America. However, the newly formed United Nations committee on refugees had determined that any ethnic Germans from Russia who had received assistance from the Nazi army were not eligible to immigrate. Through the MCC, it was decided that if these Mennonites could prove they were originally from the Netherlands and had accepted assistance to survive, then they could receive immigrant status.

Chapter 24
A House in Detmold

Not long after the soldiers' visit, Anita's family moved to the nearby town of Detmold. Her father found a better job in the city, and they rented a nice house in the suburbs. The two-story house was originally occupied by the caretaker of a larger residence. Here, for the first time, Anita had a room of her own.

Her father spent many evenings at secret meetings with agents of the Mennonite Central Committee. He had to be very cautious because communist operatives were everywhere, searching for Ukrainian refugees so they could take them to Siberia.

At home, Father instructed his family on their ancestral history for the first time. Anita learned her family had come from Dutch ancestors. Generations ago, their last name, Friesen, had been Von Riesen. When the communists took over Ukraine, the name had changed. The prefix Von indicated nobility, which was not acceptable to the communists.

Light returned to her father's eyes. There was a possibility that the

Anita and Alice

family would be able to go to Canada. Anita was even sent to take private English lessons from two ladies in Detmold. And laughter from joyful hearts enveloped their home with the birth of a new baby sister, Alice.

Between work, school, and private lessons, there was little time for play, but Rudi and Anita found a way. In their exploration, the twins discovered an abandoned military post in the forest outside of Detmold. Rummaging, they found large wheels of dried food left behind by the retreating German army, a precious commodity to a large and always hungry family. The barracks also held many fascinating photographs, magazines, and books. In the officers' quarters, Anita found beautiful treasures. She resisted the temptation to take all of them, but she did tuck a beautiful marble lion into her pocket.

Rudi and Anita stole every free moment to visit the post. The deserted machinery and equipment awed them, and they raced the small artillery wagons down a short hill. However, the adventures to their hidden paradise did not last very long. The British soldiers found out and forbade the teens from playing there. This was for their own safety—children nearby had met their deaths from defective grenades.

Anita's sisters Lene, Alice, and Katie

One day, as she and her mother worked in the garden, Anita noticed a miserable-looking soldier standing at the gate to the property. He was staring at them and looked like he was trying to decide whether to enter or not. Anita turned to tell her mother that there was a beggar at the gate, but to her surprise, her mother was running with her arms wide open toward the soldier.

It was Helmut! He had survived the war after all. They had never heard from him, and no news had arrived with his whereabouts. Yet, after months of wandering and searching, he found them. Their whole family was back together again. Anita's mother told her that God had answered her prayers, but Anita did not believe her. It made no sense. Why should God listen to her mother?

Chapter 25
Mennonite Refugee Camp

It was only a few nights later that the family's relatively peaceful life in post-war Detmold came to a close.

"Wake up, Anita," Mother said in a hushed voice. "Get dressed and come downstairs. Do not say a word or make any noise." She headed toward her sisters' bedroom.

Anita quickly got up and groped for her clothes in the darkness. Something about her mother's voice warned her to leave the lights off. Fear in her throat, she looked out of the window. Nothing stirred. It was perfectly quiet in the yard, and darkness cloaked the neighborhood.

Lightly stepping down the stairs, she joined her family gathered in the dark.

"We have to go," her father said quietly. "No one can know we are leaving. You must not make any noise. We dare not wake the neighbors."

"Can we take anything with us?" said Rudi.

"Only a coat and a small bag. Quickly, get ready, all of you. We leave in five minutes."

Anita hurried back up the stairs, feet softly padding all the way. She looked around her room, spied the beautiful lion figurine, and sadly shook her head. That treasure would have to stay. Gathering her coat, she turned to go, and stopped. The beautiful postcards she bought in Hindenburg! There, lying on the table where she left them, the beautiful faces smiled as if nothing bad ever happened. Tucking them into her waistband, she hurried out. Anita had no souvenirs from her Ukrainian village, but she would keep these treasures and store all her memories in them.

The family slipped out the door into the night. The hush of evening enveloped them as they picked their way down the dark path. It was very late, and no one in the town seemed to be awake. Even the dogs were quiet.

Baby Alice slept in her mother's arms. Anita wondered why she did not wake up. Helmut carried toddler Hansi on his back in silence. Rudi and Anita helped to steady their younger sisters, who sniffled and tried hard not to cry.

Father led the family out of the gate, turning onto a path that led behind the houses. Twisting and turning down narrow streets, they walked for several miles. No one made a sound.

Finally, they came to a high fence surrounding a large building. Father stopped them under a huge sprawling tree between two houses that backed up to the fence. Its branches hung low, concealing the family in their cover. Anita held her breath. Hearing a sniffle, she reached her arm around her little sister and held her close.

"Stay here and do not make a sound. There are people watching the gate," Father whispered.

Keeping to the shadows, he slowly moved toward the entrance. Beyond the gate, a figure stepped out of the darkness. Without moving from the shadows, Father whispered to the guard. Then, he turned and crept back to the huddled family.

"Now move, just as you saw me go, and do not talk. We are to approach the gate, and the guard will let us in," he smiled. "We are almost safe."

As quietly as they could, the family inched forward. Suddenly, lights from a nearby truck came on, flooding their route to the gate. A loud voice yelled in Russian to halt.

"Run," Father yelled. "Run to the gate!"

He did not need to say more. One and all stampeded for the gate.

The Russian agents drove their truck to block the path, their lights flashing, military orders barking. But this family, trained and hardened by dangerous events, only pressed on with more urgency. The gate opened and Anita and her family careened through, stumbling and colliding.

With a bang, the gate slammed shut behind them. The guards on the wall warned the Russians to back away. Mother collapsed to her knees, clutching the now crying baby. Father counted heads and pulled the little girls toward him. The older teens nervously chuckled and taunted the disappearing enemy. Overwhelmed and relieved, they began to laugh and chatter.

The Friesens had arrived at the refugee center of the Mennonite Central Committee in Gronau, Germany, protected by the British army and close to the border of Holland. They were finally safe and out of the Russian army's reach.

***

Anita and her family were among the fortunate. Russia demanded all Ukrainian citizens be returned. The German Vertrauensmänner had registered 35,000 Ukrainian Mennonite refugees. Of that number, 23,000 were sent back to Russia after the war ended. These were transferred by freight train to Siberia and the labor camps where only a small fraction survived.

A few thousand were able to make it to the safety of the Allied occupied areas and the protected refugee camps. Those who made it to safe havens under protection of the British or Americans had to wait in hopes of finding a country that would allow them to immigrate.

The Mennonite Central Committee was able to arrange immigration status for some 3,000 Mennonite refugees in the country of Paraguay. The refugees were allotted land for colonies and the freedom to organize schools, churches, and some degree of self-governance. All of this was organized and funded by generous Mennonites in the United States and Canada.

Chapter 26
The *Charlton Monarch*—1948

After weeks of waiting, Anita's family finally received permission to immigrate to Paraguay. They would be given a plot of land and a chance to build a new home and start a new life. Anita was thoroughly excited. The new world and its mysteries enticed her. At seventeen years old, she couldn't wait to leave the boring refugee camp life behind.

Anita had never even seen the ocean, and now she was going to be a passenger on the British ship *Charlton Monarch* and journey across the sea to South America. The trip would take two to three weeks, but waiting to board seemed to take forever. The ship was supposed to leave in April 1948 for Buenos Aires, Brazil, but four delays due to maintenance issues pushed the date further and further. Finally, on May 16, the boat left the port of Bremerhaven with 860 Mennonite refugees on board.

It didn't take long for Anita and the other passengers to realize that the *Charlton Monarch* was not built for comfort. It was a British freighter that had been converted into a troop transport for the war. There were huge rooms fitted with bunk beds, one room for the married women and children, one for the single young women, and others for the men and boys. Another huge room was piped with multiple showerheads—with no curtains for privacy. The dining room was a great hall with wooden tables and benches in long rows. Still, Anita and the other teens found many places to explore and chances to get in trouble with the crew and leaders of the Mennonite Central Committee. Elfrieda Dyck, the MCC leader in charge, was always expecting mischief. Of course, the teens learned how to avoid her watchful eye.

But getting caught was the least of their concerns onboard the *Charlton Monarch*. Leaving Bremerhaven, the ship only traveled as far as Rotterdam, Holland, about 200 miles, before it had to stop for another delay with engine trouble. At this point, some of the ship's engineering crew left, refusing to sail on a vessel in such poor condition.

But the captain called for replacements from the ship's company in London, and off they went again. At least ten times over eight days the engines stopped, causing the power to go off. Without lights and refrigeration, the crew and passengers became increasingly frustrated. On May 28, they pulled into port at the Cape Verde Islands, just off the coast of Africa, with no electricity, no fresh water for drinking, and no salt water for toilets. While remaining there six days for repairs, about half the passengers came down with food poisoning since there was no refrigeration for the meat.

Anita tried to find silver linings amid the misery. Often in charge of her little sisters, she would collect a group of children and organize games to keep them occupied. Other times, she volunteered to distribute the used clothing and toys that the Canadian Mennonites had donated for the refugees. When the engines stopped, as they often did, some of the older teens headed topside and watched for sharks. As the ship drifted, sharks gathered, especially when scraps were thrown overboard. The teens made it a competition to see how many sharks they could count as they leaned over the railing.

Chapter 27
Adrift

It was four thirty in the morning when the sound of hissing woke Anita. She was accustomed to the silence that enveloped the ship after the engines stopped—but this time felt different. The ship rocked back and forth, and she could tell that the sea winds blew strongly. Without the engines, she knew the ship was helpless against the waves. She supposed that the hissing noise was coming from the steam engines. Others around her stirred as well, and concerned voices sounded increasingly alarmed.

"Turn on the light," someone shouted.

She heard the click of the switch, but there was no response.

Of course, Anita thought. *The power's out again.*

"It's the boilers, they've blown," another groaned.

It was pitch black inside the sleeping hall. Anita groped about until she found her clothes and shoes and felt her way to the door. She wanted to know what was happening outside. Gripping the railing tightly, she made her way up the stairs, reeling back and forth as the ship swayed. She could feel the strong winds tearing at the hatchway. She knew she wasn't supposed to go above deck in the dark, but at this moment even the dim light from the stars made it worth the risk.

Once outside, she could see the crew rushing about. She grabbed the rail and steadied herself against the wind. The waves crashed hard against the ship, and cold sea spray shocked her face. It was obvious that the ship was in trouble. Every few minutes a flare rocketed into the sky, an SOS to signal any nearby boats.

Looking about, she saw many with their heads bowed. Some cried, and others gazed upward with their hands raised.

What's the use of praying? Anita thought. *If there is a god, he doesn't care about us.*

Her years of school had taught her to doubt God. Even if He was there, she trusted herself. Wasn't she strong enough to handle any situation on her own? She didn't need Him, did she?

Hours passed as the ship drifted, dipping side to side and end to end. By morning, the wind and waves had subsided somewhat, and the captain had set the rudder so the ship appeared to spin. The wake of the ship left an arc in the water, which closed into a circle as the day dawned.

As the sky brightened with the morning, Anita could see that the rails were lined with frightened passengers. Some preferred to hide in the dark halls away from the wind, but most were on the deck, if only to escape the nausea that came with the tossing ship and the stench of overflowing toilets.

"Look at that circle in the water. We're in a maelstrom," said one of Anita's friends. "I saw a picture of one in a book. We're caught in it, and we have no power! We're doomed!"

Anita had seen pictures in storybooks and read about whirlpools that caught ships and restrained them until they disappeared to the bottom of the ocean. Suddenly fear choked her throat, and her heart began to race. Prayer—should she pray?

Word passed from person to person that a meeting was being held down below. Anita assumed they were gathering to pray, but she preferred to stay on deck and watch. Most of the other teens stayed topside as well, imagining the circle getting smaller and smaller and counting sharks to pretend they weren't scared.

A little later, Anita discovered what the adults had learned at the meeting. They were indeed in a dangerous situation, about 100 miles off the coast of Brazil. The engines were in bad shape, and the boat floated near shallow waters, where rocks were an extreme hazard. The ship's radio equipment was also in poor repair and unable to reach far enough to get help. The engineers were working to make repairs, but the prospect looked dim. They were not, however, caught in a maelstrom, despite what the overexcited teens believed.

Several tense days of watching and worrying followed. Water had to be rationed, and there was never enough. Amplified by the stinking toilet situation, seasickness was rampant—especially at night when the passengers lay in darkness, listening to the creaking and groaning of the helpless ship.

Finally, an emergency transmitter reached the *John Biscoy*, a small steamship fifty miles away. The ship responded immediately and arrived at ten o'clock that night. Since the waves were too high to risk attaching tow lines, the boat stayed close in case of further danger. By the early morning of June 12, tow lines were attached, and the *John Biscoy* towed the *Charlton Monarch* for twelve hours until they reached the city of Recife in the state of Pernambuco, Brazil.

Safe harbor was a big relief, but the weary passengers of the *Charlton* were still 2,500 miles from their destination. It would take another month before the ship could be repaired.

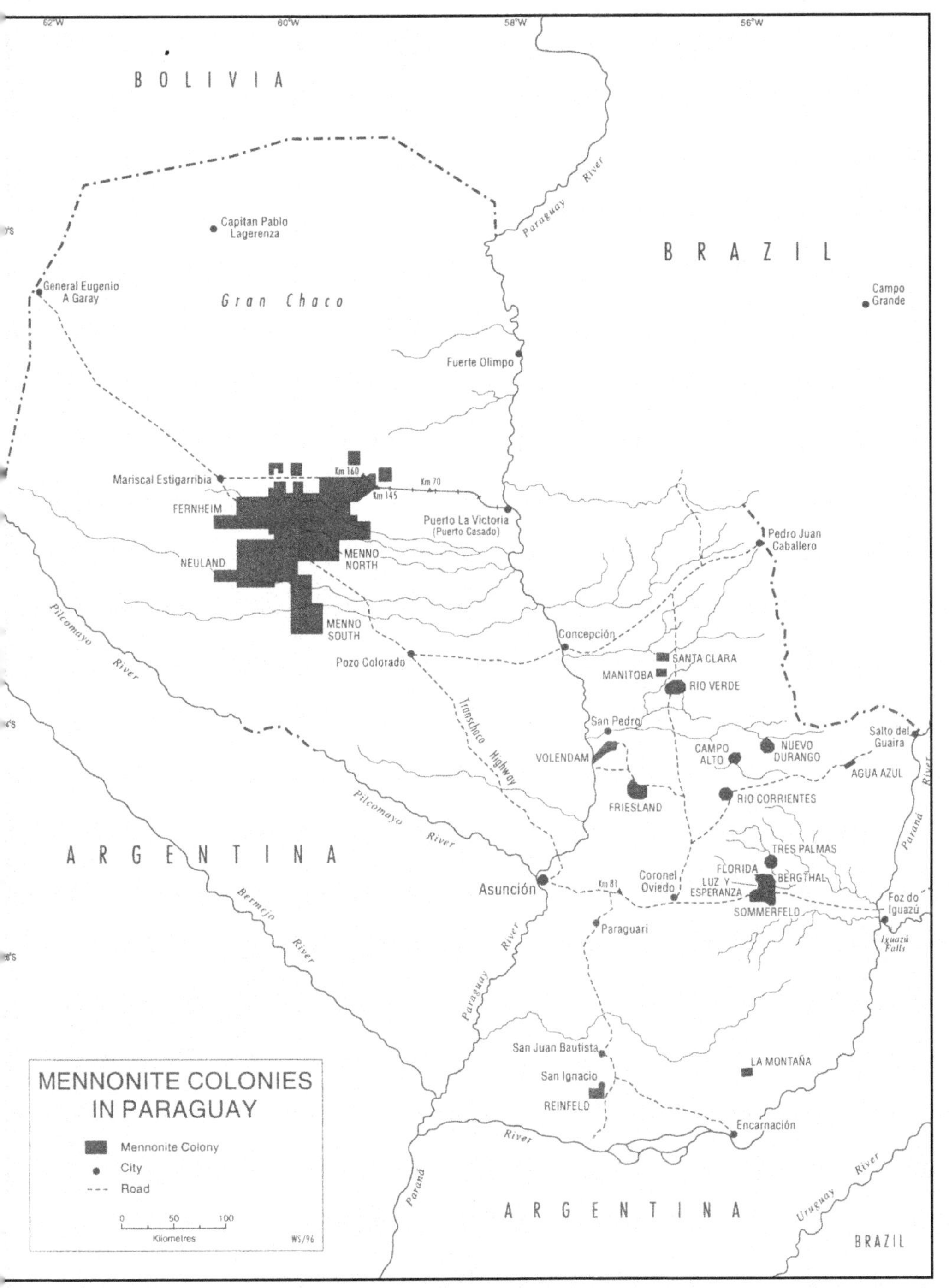

62°W
60°W
58°W
56°W
BOLIVIA
Capitan Pablo
Lagerenza
General Eugenio
A Garay
Gran Chaco
BRAZIL
Campo
Grande
Fuerte Olimpo
Paraguay River
Mariscal Estigarribia
Km 160
Km 70
Km 145
FERNHEIM
Puerto La Victoria
(Puerto Casado)
Pedro Juan
Caballero
NEULAND
MENNO
NORTH
MENNO
SOUTH
Pilcomayo River
Pozo Colorado
Concepción
SANTA CLARA
MANITOBA
RIO VERDE
San Pedro
Transchaco Highway
VOLENDAM
CAMPO
ALTO
NUEVO
DURANGO
Salto del
Guaira
AGUA AZUL
Pilcomayo River
FRIESLAND
RIO CORRIENTES
Paraná River
ARGENTINA
TRES PALMAS
Bermejo River
Asunción
Km 81
Coronel
Oviedo
FLORIDA
LUZ Y
ESPERANZA
BERGTHAL
SOMMERFELD
Foz do
Iguazú
Paraguay River
Paraguari
Iguazú
Falls
San Juan Bautista
LA MONTAÑA
San Ignacio
REINFELD
Encarnación
Parana River
Uruguay River
ARGENTINA
Parana River
BRAZIL
MENNONITE COLONIES
IN PARAGUAY
Mennonite Colony
City
Road
0
50
100
Kilometres
WS/96

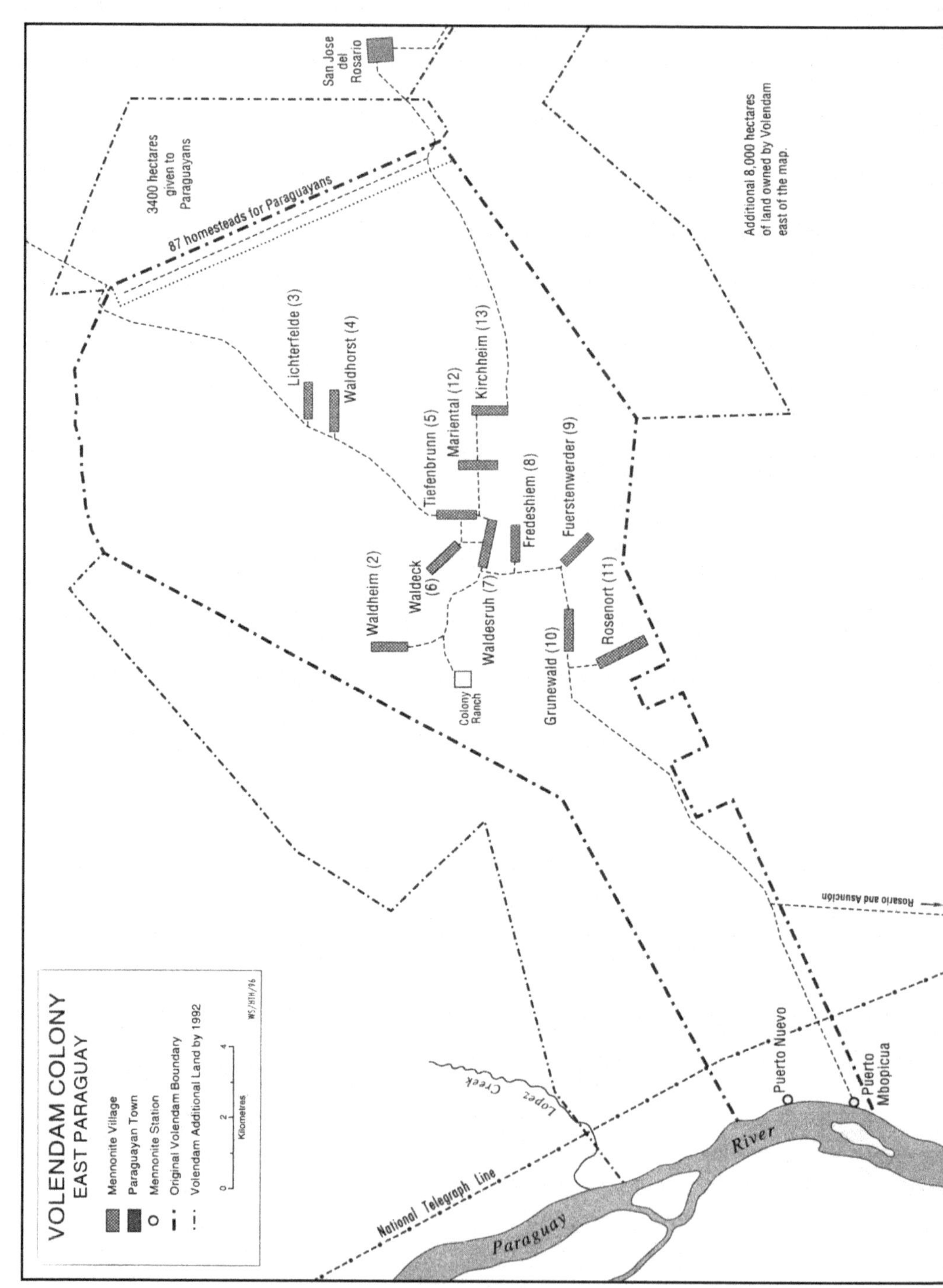
San Jose del Rosario
3400 hectares given to Paraguayans
87 homesteads for Paraguayans
Additional 8,000 hectares of land owned by Volendam east of the map.
Lichterfelde (3)
Waldhorst (4)
Mariental (12)
Kirchheim (13)
Tiefenbrunn (5)
Fredeshiem (8)
Fuerstenwerder (9)
Waldheim (2)
Waldeck (6)
Waldesruh (7)
Rosenort (11)
Grunewald (10)
Colony Ranch
Rosario and Asunción
Lopez Creek
Puerto Nuevo
Puerto Mbopicua
River
National Telegraph Line
Paraguay
VOLENDAM COLONY
EAST PARAGUAY
Mennonite Village
Paraguayan Town
Mennonite Station
Original Volendam Boundary
Volendam Additional Land by 1992
WS/JH1H/96
0   2   4
Kilometres

Chapter 28
Paraguay

Because of the delay, the Mennonite Central Committee took small groups of refugees to their destinations by plane. Most were sent to the Chaco, a desert plain where even the hardworking Mennonites could barely survive.

Fortunately for Anita's family, one of their relatives had arrived in Paraguay on a previous ship and settled in the Volendam colony, established in a jungle area. So, the Friesens—Gerhard, Katharina, Arnold, Helmut, Rudi, Anita, Lene, Katie, Hansi, and Alice—all boarded a plane for Asunción, Paraguay.

Asunción, an inland port on the Paraguay River, was still many miles from their destination. From there, the weary family traveled by boat upriver to the smaller village of Villa del Rosario. It was late at night when they pulled into port. Anita stood along the rail as the boat eased its way to the rickety dock. A half-dressed man approached to tie the ropes to a mooring post.

Suddenly, Anita felt dizzy. The dock was moving! She tried to concentrate. No, it wasn't the dock. It was something else that dispersed in waves ahead of the man as he walked.Next to her, one of the crew laughed, "Look at those cockroaches!"

Anita shrank back from the rail, horrified. The whole dock was covered with cockroaches in the darkness, and they scrambled underneath the boards when the man approached.

So, this is Paraguay, she thought to herself. *Germany was so much better. They didn't have cockroaches there. Why did we come here? This is no place for someone like me.*

Years of schooling under Stalin and Hitler had convinced Anita that she was important to the future of her country and that her parents were insignificant and useless. She had been told that she was exceptional, destined to have an important job, live in a modern apartment, and serve a grand purpose. Paraguay, with its dusty streets and backward jungles, was never part of her dreams.

Nevertheless, she had no choice but to follow her family off the boat and toward a refugee center, where they would spend the night. They carried what they could, but most of their bags were left on board to be delivered in the morning. Exhausted, they settled in for a few hours of sleep wherever they could find an empty chair.

Early the next morning, they piled onto several horse-drawn wagons headed inland to the Volendam colony. Their bags and supplies had disappeared. The few tools, kitchen utensils, and clothing they had left behind the night before were all stolen, leaving them nothing but what they had managed to carry the night before.

Even in the tropics, the temperature by the sea and river was tolerable. The jungle heat, however, was unbearable. The humidity drained Anita of what little energy she had, and the bugs tormented her. The makeshift road was a "corduroy" one, constructed of logs laid side by side, which made for endless thumping as the wagons lurched along.

Hours of tropical heat, insects, and teeth-shattering bumps finally brought them to a small village named Tiefenbrunn and Aunt Marisha's tiny thatch-covered house. Gratefully, the children tumbled off the wagon and greeted their aunt, relieved to have reached the end of their long journey but rather uneasy about their jungle surroundings.

The first night was terrifying. Howling monkeys, a jaguar's scream, the constant roar of insects, and a multitude of other sounds kept Anita awake most of the night. Not that it mattered. There were no beds available—only a chair to curl up in. She pulled it close to the smoky fire that helped keep the insects and wild animals away. Exhausted as she was, the night sounds nearly drove her crazy.

There was no rest for the weary family. Early the next day, as the newcomers began to take stock of their environment, Anita's father realized that beds to keep them off the ground were the priority. He and the boys set off to cut saplings and learn the art of jungle furniture making.

After gathering heaps of sticks, they arranged four thick branches for bedposts and then latched on sturdy cross timbers with many saplings laid between. A trip to the pampas grassland secured thatch that was distributed over the bedframes. The Mennonite Central Committee cooperative in the village provided blankets that were then laid over the thatch. Hardly perfect but serviceable, the beds were arranged on the dirt floor under the porch roof.

That evening, Anita eyed the bed cautiously, too tired to complain. She settled in, covered her head with a corner of the blanket, and soon fell asleep, completely exhausted.

The next thing she knew, she awoke to the sound of giggling. All her siblings were gathered around her, laughing. Disoriented at first, she realized that during the night, the saplings in her less-than-perfect bed had split apart, and she had slipped onto the dirt.

"What's so funny?" Her groggy voice made them giggle all the more. "At least the ground is smoother than those branches."

"Maybe so," said Rudi, before he chuckled again. "Oh, Anita, it sure was nice of you to share your bed with a friend!"

"What?" said Anita with a start. She sat up quickly. There, cuddled up next to her, was a small pink piglet, stretched out luxuriously in the folds of her blanket. Anita screamed, the piglet squealed, and howls of laughter echoed through the jungle.

Chapter 29
Home in the Jungle

Just a few days later, Anita's father arranged to buy a plot at the end of Tiefenbrunn. It was a piece of the jungle like the rest, but it was a piece they could call home.

Early the next morning, the family was roused out of a restless sleep to begin clearing the land. The older boys were given machetes— long, sturdy knives—to chop away the bushes, vines, and shrubs. Anita and the younger girls transferred the chopped vegetation to large piles that would be burned. Father and Arnold used axes to fell whatever trees they could.

The jungle heat was intense, draining the energy from their muscles and shortening their tempers. Without gloves, it wasn't long before all

Left to right: Katie, Alice, Anita, Hansi, and Lene in Paraguay

complained of blisters, but that was the least of their concerns. Dripping with sweat from head to toe, the family was an irresistible target for mosquitoes and other insects. To add to their misery, the jungle foliage blocked most of the wind, so the air felt steamy. It was exhausting work.

Even with numb hands and minds blurred by fatigue, they had to watch for dangerous jungle animals. Snakes seemed to be everywhere, hiding among the vines and bushes, ready to strike the human invaders. High in the canopy, monkeys howled warnings and occasionally threw sticks and fruit. The threat of deadly insects, spiders, and army ants lurked at every turn. Anita knew that jaguars, tapirs, land crocodiles, wild cattle, and other unfamiliar animals wandered about, frightening these newcomers from Europe.

The jungle did not give up its territory easily. But little by little, chop by chop, the family hacked out a space of their own. Each day the space got larger until they finally began the construction of a small house.

With wood brought from the Mennonite Central Committee sawmill on the Paraná River, the men and boys shaped the house's internal skeleton. In the plans, it only had a few rooms, but a veranda spanned the length, providing additional shade. Once the structure was framed, the tough work of making adobe bricks began.

The girls, once again, had an important job to do. Shoeless, they stomped in the mud pits where dirt, straw, and cow dung were combined. Once the mixture looked smooth, they scooped it up with their hands and filled the wooden molds. Laid in the hot jungle sun, the bricks soon dried hard and were removed from the molds. These bricks would be stacked to form the sturdy walls of their new home.

Next, it was time for a trip to the pampas. The shoulder-high grass was perfect for cutting and layering onto the crossbeams of the roof. A two-hour wagon trip brought the family to a large area where pampas grass grew the tallest. This time, even Anita had a large machete to slice away. This was backbreaking work in the most stifling conditions, especially since she had to wear long sleeves as protection from the sharp grass. Bending, slicing, and gathering the bundles for hours was tough enough, but the extreme temperatures and tall grasses prevented even the slightest breeze. Of course, there were also the dangers of poisonous snakes, feral hogs, and wild cattle that hid in the grass. Anita checked in all directions for snakes—these were not the little ones from her childhood that she loved to catch. These could kill.

For once, Anita looked forward to the long, bumpy wagon ride home, and she appreciated the evening's rest gathered around the smoky bonfire that kept mosquitos away. This was a time for storytelling and laughter as shared hardships gave rise to warm fellowship. Anita discovered she had a knack for telling exciting stories and often entertained the younger children until they fell asleep.

Within a few months, the Friesen family had carved out a reasonably comfortable home. With help from neighbors and the accumulated wisdom of the Guarani people, they cultivated fruit trees and a garden of their own. Before long, they had planted fields of manioc (a starchy vegetable) and peanuts. A pigpen and a chicken coop were added to the yard along with dogs for protection and a cow to provide milk and cheese. Guinea fowl, known for their loud calls, provided an early warning system against snakes.

Anita hated the jungle, hated the heat, hated the bugs, and, most of all, hated the sweat. Yet, even though the labor was exhausting, she had to admit that it was satisfying to work with her family as they created

Anita and calf

a home out of this inhospitable place. Nevertheless, she desperately wanted to leave the jungle and go back to the familiar conveniences of the city.

Chapter 30
Lessons from the Jungle

Anita soon realized that the jungle had plenty to teach her steppe-raised family. Their farming background served them well as they learned to navigate the new environment. Fortunately, the indigenous people helped the first settlers understand which crops flourished, and each season brought deeper understanding.

Peanuts, unfamiliar to the family, quickly became a staple of their diet. A room in the house was designated for the freshly dug plants. There, the peanuts dried until the whole family joined in a "peanut party" as they separated the nuts from the roots. Even the dogs got involved, snapping up any peanuts that fell to the ground.

Another native plant, manioc, served as a primary food source for the indigenous population. It was a dependable crop, but it had to be prepared carefully. Otherwise, Anita and her family would suffer the consequences of multiple trips to the outhouse—or worse.

Of course, the amenities weren't pleasant to begin with. The outhouse was a smelly, three-sided affair with a strip of burlap hanging in front. It stood some distance from the house and backed up to the banana grove. Anita was forbidden to enter the grove because snakes and tarantulas hid in the leaves there. Plenty of critters already visited the outhouse, so a trek to the bathroom was its own adventure.

Anita's brothers learned new skills to hunt in the jungle. A wild pig hunt demanded extreme tree-climbing abilities when the hunters became the hunted. For catching monkeys, the boys brought an umbrella. Monkey "rain" was very unpleasant.

The hunters always carried machetes as valuable weapons and tools.

Snakes often raided the henhouse in search of eggs, but they were no match for the machetes. Even caimans, or "land crocs," fell victim when these five-foot-long reptiles entered the coop. Fortunately, the guinea fowl were excellent security guards that alerted everyone to invaders.

Even the smallest creatures presented a danger to the unaware. Sand fleas were everywhere, often embedding themselves under toenails. Each night, the family soaked their feet to prevent infection from flea nests. The hard clay floor of the house stayed wet to keep the flea population down—but it didn't stop the huge red ants that marched through their home, vicious if anyone stood in their way. Screwworms also frequently burrowed into their skin, hiding in boils that had to be squeezed for removal.

The big tapir that foraged in their garden did not pose a threat to the family—just the vegetables. The cattle that roamed the jungle, however, were extremely dangerous. The large Brahman bulls or zebu with their humped backs and sharp horns wandered freely, and they had quite the temper. The village road was fenced on both sides to keep cattle from straying into the yards.

Other dangers also required vigilance, but they were not impossible to overcome. For Anita and her family, nature's threats were far more manageable than the terrible circumstances they had miraculously escaped.

Chapter 31
Adventure

Anita missed the beauty of the German countryside and the conveniences of the city. She wanted nothing to do with the hard work of jungle life, yet the excitement of the unknown was thrilling. However, the possibilities of what lay around the trail bend often drew her into danger.

One morning, Anita awoke from her lumpy bed to the sound of toucans fighting in the papaya tree. Knowing how important the fruit was, she stepped outside to throw sticks at the birds. Her mother usually banged loudly on pots and pans, but it was too early in the morning for such noise.

She headed for the outhouse but stopped to watch a huge frog walking—not hopping—down the path. These comical frogs always caught her attention. She usually stepped around the giant spiders on her route, but the foot-long frogs were worth watching.

Back home, she saw her mother on the big veranda, straining to get some meat down. It was hung from a beam on the porch's edge to dry. Anita helped her reach it, holding the meat while her mother scraped the maggots off. She sniffed disgustedly but knew this was the only way to preserve meat without electricity.

Meanwhile, Anita watched as her mother's pet coatimundi snuffled around the corners of the veranda. It was a funny little animal with a long snout and curious habits. However, it was as loyal as any dog she had ever known. Her mother had raised it from infancy, and now it followed her everywhere, even curling up in her lap.After breakfast, Anita planned to visit a neighbor down the road, but first she took a short walk in the jungle. This was one of her favorite things to do early in the morning. She did not go far, but she loved testing her courage with a hike into the wild, often joined by her only dog, Boquerón.

The dog usually stayed close to her, but this morning Boquerón seemed to have other things on his mind. He followed her a short while but later diverted from the jungle path. Anita made as little noise as possible, hoping to see a small creature like an armadillo or coatimundi.

Suddenly, she froze. There, about ten feet away, was a jaguar looking straight at her. Where was Boquerón? For several seconds, the girl and the cat stared into each other's eyes. The jaguar appeared to be determining if she was a threat— or considering how she would

Anita and Boquerón in Tiefenbrunn

taste. Anita didn't move a muscle. Instinct told her not to run. After a few moments, the cat turned and walked away.

Just then, Boquerón bolted through the brush barking frantically. Startled, the cat ran after the dog in hot pursuit.

"Boquerón! Come back!" Anita shouted. She knew he was no match for the cat. It took a minute or two, but the dog finally returned, panting and proud of himself for saving his mistress.

This was not the only rescue he pulled off that day. Just an hour later Anita left to visit her friend. She crossed the fence onto the road, unaware that a large Brahman bull was nearby. The bull, agitated by the barking dog, snorted, lowered its head, and charged toward her.

"Boquerón!" Anita screamed as she sprinted for the fence, the bull not far behind. Out of the corner of her eye, she saw the little dog racing toward the bull. Reaching the fence, she dove and rolled under the bottom log. Boquerón knew what to do. He leaped straight at the bull's face and clamped his teeth on the loose skin that hung below its head. The bull bellowed and stomped, swinging its head from side to side. But the determined canine held on tight, swinging wildly back and forth while the bull thrashed and bucked.

Finally, Boquerón's grip loosened, and he flew to the side. The bull bellowed and rushed toward him, but Boquerón raced under the fence to find Anita sitting on the ground, safe. Hugging the trembling little dog, she gave him all the attention he deserved, grateful for such a faithful friend.

Chapter 32
A Rebellious Heart

For the young people of the community, Saturday was a day of fun-filled excursions and youth meetings. Occasionally, they organized a two-hour wagon trip to swim in the river. No one seemed to mind that they shared the river with caimans and piranha. As long as the humans kept their distance, the crocodiles remained basking on an island in the middle of the river. The piranha stayed cautious around activity and only attacked if they sensed blood. Even with these threats, the tropic heat was enough to drive the reckless teens into the cool water.

On Saturday evenings, the Mennonite youth met for a time of fellowship. They played games, ate peanuts and homemade candy, and sang around a bonfire. There were two different gatherings the teens could choose from. The Mennonite Brethren sponsored a youth group that included Bible study while the general Mennonites focused on entertainment. Anita chose the fun group. She had no desire for Bible study. That was boring and, in her mind, useless. Her brother Helmut was more serious about spiritual pursuits. He encouraged Anita to consider deeper matters of faith, but she was not interested.

The village held church each Sunday morning in a cleared-out area of the jungle. Logs were laid down in rows for the people to sit on. Occasionally, a snake joined the congregation and slithered through the seats, causing a commotion among the ladies. Most stepped out of the way and let the visitor pass quietly. Anita always laughed, happy to see the solemn church service disrupted by the disrespectful villain.

As part of the Mennonite community, she tried to fit in and fulfill expectations. She joined the church choir, attended catechism, and

Oxcart in Paraguay

committed herself to the church in a ceremony where she was sprinkled with water, representing baptism. Yet she resented the church's values more and more. She decided that the Mennonite leaders were hypocrites, teaching others to be humble and obedient while they were arrogant and selfish.

"When you point a finger at someone, three fingers point back," her mother often said. Increasingly, Anita applied that principle to the village leaders, forgetting that it also applied to herself.

The Mennonite community maintained high expectations for their youth. Hard work, obedience, humility, and compliance to the Mennonite standards were considered duties. There were many rules, and Anita hated them all. As a child, she had been trained by the philosophies of Stalin and Hitler. She had learned to obey government leadership and ignore the teachings of family and church. Religion was part of the old way, and her generation was destined to lead the world into innovation and prosperity.

Once, as she wandered on a jungle trail near her home, she stopped to observe a large yellow snake shedding its old skin. As it left its worn-out scales, the snake emerged glistening with colors brighter than before. *I want to be like that snake*, she thought. *I want to leave this life behind and find a new life.*

"I will never marry a Mennonite," she declared vehemently to the sky. "I'm going to marry an American and leave this place and these stuffy hypocrites. America will give me freedom from these useless rules!"

Chapter 33
A New Job

In 1948, a small, primitive hospital was established in the village, headed by a proud German doctor. Because of Anita's training in Hitler Youth, the doctor asked her to help at the facility and learn to be a nurse. She accepted the job. At eighteen, she worked in patient care, administration of medicines, and recordkeeping.

The clerical work, often done at night, was anything but dull. The hospital had screens to keep the mosquitoes out, but little jungle frogs managed to find their way inside. Attracted by a lantern light on the desk, the tree frogs were frequent visitors as Anita worked on the record books. In the darkness, they crept up and jumped at sudden movements. Anita liked it. She snickered when they leaped at her pencil as she wrote.

This job suited her, but the arrogant doctor did not. She often led the other nurses to prank the old doctor, even once putting laxatives in his drink.

Despite her mischievous nature, Anita excelled at her work, gaining the trust of the doctor and patients alike. One young woman came from a nearby Paraguayan ranch for assistance in

Jungle hospital

childbirth. Anita attended her, quickly earning her friendship. Two months later, the young woman invited Anita to a fiesta at the ranch as thanks for her care.

Thrilled for a chance to leave the village, Anita set out on the journey with Helmut along as a guide and protector. The ride on horseback took several hours, but for Anita, the excitement of the unknown made the travel worth it.

The ranch, or *estancia* as it is called in Spanish, was a large cattle operation. It included an imposing hacienda and several typical outbuildings, all beautifully decorated for the fiesta. Gauchos on silver-bedecked saddles arrived along with other guests, all dressed for a party. The young mother greeted Helmut and Anita with gracious formality and treated them to a special luncheon in the hacienda's dining room. For once, the normally talkative Anita kept quiet, not only because she could not speak Spanish, but also because the formal setting was overwhelming for a girl accustomed to dirt-floor feasting.

Anita

The fiesta began that evening as guests were treated to Paraguayan barbeque. Each sliced off a piece of meat from beef roasting over a firepit. Music filled the air as the *peons*, local peasants hired by the ranch, played their guitars and serenaded the guests. Anita was enchanted by the extravagance of the boisterous party. It was so much more interesting than the quiet, sober events of the steadfast Mennonites. She happily joined in the festivities while Helmut kept a watchful eye from the sidelines.

The ride home that next morning brought out the worst in the frustrated Anita.

"Helmut, I'm nothing like these Mennonites," she said all at once, the words bursting from her heart. "I can't stay here in this jungle. Can't you see that? I'll go to the city, I'll get a job, I'll find an American, marry him, and travel across the sea and never come back to this boring backwater place again."

Helmut sighed. "That's not going to happen, Anita."

He glanced at her and hesitated, then smiled as he pointed at the trees. "There are no Americans around here, just monkeys. Take your pick."

There was a silence before Helmut spoke again. This time he was serious.

"Really, Anita, can't you just be grateful that you are alive? Don't you remember what we came through to get to Paraguay? God took care of us. We were brought here for a reason."

"God? Does God want me to rot here in this jungle? I'll never be happy here." She felt her heart clenching.

"You can't run from God," Helmut said.

"Yes, I can."

And with that, neither spoke another word for the rest of the journey.

After her twentieth birthday, Anita decided that she had waited long enough and informed her parents that she was leaving for the city.

"I don't belong here. Everybody knows that but you," she told her parents. "You've seen how they treat me. I'm not like the other girls here. They call me 'gypsy girl.' They say I'm a rotten Hitler kid. So, I'm going to the city. There's a hospital there that wants me, and I can be a surgical nurse."

She raised a finger. "Don't try to make me stay here. I would sooner die than settle for an old Mennonite husband. A wagon and horses will be offered for me—and I will never accept that. I'm not a slave, and I won't be sold like I'm someone's property!"

With that, Anita took off for a new life in the city, giving no further thought to the past, people, or place she left behind.

***

Anita's parents knew she was right. The training from Stalin and Hitler had taken deep hold of her heart, and they realized she would not be satisfied with the quiet life of the Mennonites. So, Gerhard and Katharina released their hold on this headstrong daughter, giving her the freedom she so desperately longed for.

Chapter 34
Asunción

The city of Asunción lay south of the Volendam colony. It was the only real city in Paraguay, serving as the center of culture, business, and education in the country. Several Mennonite churches were located there along with numerous Mennonite businesses, schools, and the Mennonite Central Committee headquarters, so Anita knew her parents felt that she would be safe.

The doctor from the village clinic recommended Anita to work at a private maternity hospital for wealthy Germans. It was quite a distance from her apartment, which was rented from a family friend, but she rode the trolley to get there. She began to study Spanish, her fifth language, and soon worked as a translator alongside nursing. It was a good beginning, but not quite what Anita had in mind. She befriended local Paraguayans, which displeased the haughty hospital staff. Once again, Anita disregarded the norms of her Mennonite community and applied for work outside of their influence. The local Catholic hospital quickly accepted her because of her German background.

City street in Asunción

The Cruz Roja was a beautiful hospital in an old Spanish mission in Asunción. It was run by the Catholic Church and staffed by nuns. The facility served both the rich and poor of the city with the wealthy patrons on the upper floor and the poor in the basement.

The hospital's Mother Superior was Hungarian and extremely strict, demanding that Anita attend chapel each day and sing in the choir. She was determined to convert Anita to Catholicism. The woman insisted that there be no laughter in the hospital halls. Sadly, Anita and her friend, Hermana Marta, were caught laughing in the kitchen, and Marta was fired from being the cook.

It was a busy season for Anita, and she worked extremely hard. Her duties included general nursing, clerical work, and emergency care, leaving little time for sleep. Her efforts caught the eye of the head surgeon, Professor Ruiz, and before long she was asked to be his personal assistant. To Anita's delight, he authorized her for surgical training, and she became an instrumentalist, assisting in operations. She also joined the professor as he made house calls to wealthy patients and, for a time, served as the personal attendant to his wife, who was very ill with cancer.

However, Anita soon realized that her work ethic was not the only reason the professor wanted her as an assistant. Occasionally, he would put his arm around her and ask for a kiss. Assuming he was just being friendly, she usually laughed and pushed him away. But eventually it became obvious that he was serious, and Anita did the one sensible thing she could—she slapped the elderly professor.

He was not the only man who tried to take advantage of her. There were several others, and quite a few were priests. One even left the priesthood, hoping she would marry him. Anita was not impressed. She knew of several nuns who had given birth to children fathered by a priest. This was just another example of hypocrisy in the church, and she wanted none of it. She was set on getting an American husband— preferably not a religious one.

Chapter 35
An American Marine

The few Americans in Asunción were usually found near the U.S. embassy. Anita had a good friend named Suzi who worked for a Marine stationed there. It just so happened that the embassy was down the street from the Cruz Roja, and since Anita and Suzi spent a lot of time together, it wasn't too difficult for Anita to frequent the area in hopes of a chance meeting.

American Embassy in Asunción

Sure enough, one day as they passed by the embassy, a young man noticed her and politely greeted her. A few days later, while she and Suzi sat on the steps of a nearby building, he stopped and greeted her again. This time he asked her to dinner.

She looked up to bright blue eyes and wavy brown hair belonging to a handsome man dressed in a suit. He was, in fact, an American. His polite and serious demeanor gave the impression of a trustworthy and kind character. So, without a second thought, she said, "Sure."

A few days later, Don Barber, a Marine assigned to the embassy, came to pick her up for their date. Anita was surprised when he opened the car door for her. She had never ridden in a nice car before—only trains, trucks, and trolleys.

Enchanted by his nice manners and polite conversation—and by the padded car seats—Anita was shocked when they arrived at the most elegant restaurant in Asunción. She noticed everything. The restaurant was built out over the Paraná River, and its construction featured glass walls and a glass ceiling. The Southern Cross shone above them as thousands of stars twinkled in the night sky. Elegant waiters attended to their every desire, bringing food that was as beautiful as it was delicious. She had never experienced anything like it. Even the music was romantic, a soothing sound from the crooning crocodiles that resided under the restaurant.

Before dinner was over, the conversation shifted to future plans.

"Anita, would you like to go to America?" asked Don.

"Sure, everybody wants to go to America," she answered without hesitation.

"Good, then would you marry me?"

She laughed. "Sure."

"Well, then!" Don slapped his hand on the table, swelling with happiness. "I'll pick you up tomorrow morning and take you to the embassy. We have a lot of paperwork to do."

And just like that, without so much as a kiss or even a proper introduction, Anita was   engaged to be married to an American Marine. She felt like her dream was finally within grasp.

That night, she hurriedly wrote a letter to her brothers. They kept saying she'd have to choose a monkey to marry since she wouldn't marry a villager. With a glint in her eye, Anita penned a single sentence and had it sent.

The letter read, "I got my monkey!"

Chapter 36
Marriage—1953

The next morning, Don arrived to take her to the embassy. The building was a beautiful colonial-style place, gated and guarded by Marines. To Anita, it was like a palace with its shiny tiled floors and elegant furnishings. She felt a bit nervous, but the diplomats and officers were courteous and kind. They informed Don that Americans were not allowed to marry Paraguayans, but since Anita had a German background, they could cancel her citizenship and draw up new papers. With a wink and

American Embassy in Asunción

a nod, permission was granted, and the engagement was settled.

The next few months became a flurry of activity for Anita. She had a physical, blood tests, and X-rays done to qualify for the immigration papers, along with a multitude of vaccinations.

Her work at the hospital continued for a time, but she was soon asked to help at the embassy as a translator. In the midst of all her duties, she arranged for a seamstress to make a wedding dress. Her friend, Anni Stein, who worked at a nearby store, helped her plan the wedding and organized a bridal shower. In fact, there would be two weddings. In Paraguay, the law required a civil wedding officiated by a judge, but her

Don and friends

family required a church wedding, so they planned to have both.

The night of the bridal shower, Don took off work to spend some time with the ambassador. He asked his friend, Bill, to guard the gate in his absence. That night, there was trouble outside the gate with Paraguayan rebels. Shots were fired, and Bill was wounded. Anita felt terrible for Bill but knew that her fiancé had narrowly avoided a dangerous situation. He could have been killed and all her plans shattered in a moment. She had so little control. She wondered if she needed to thank God for saving him. Did God have a bigger purpose for Don?

She didn't dwell on "what could have been" and "what ifs" for long. There was too much to occupy her mind. On June 6, 1953, Anita and Don were married in front of a judge and two legal witnesses. The cer-

Wedding photo with Ambassador Shaw

emony was held in a beautiful villa across the street from the embassy. Many of the embassy staff were there to celebrate with them, including Ambassador George P. Shaw.

A week later, Anita and Don took passage on a small boat headed upriver toward her family's village of Tiefenbrunn. Curiously, the boat was named the *Santa Anita*. It had four cabins above deck, one of which the young couple shared with several other passengers. Below deck, many native Paraguayans and the less affluent *peons* were housed in one large area along with pigs, goats, and other animals. It was noisy and very smelly below, but above deck the breeze off the river made for a pleasant trip.

All night they chugged slowly up the river until, early in the morning, they arrived at the small port of Mbopicuá. The ship was too large to come alongside the dock, so Anita and Don were instructed to climb aboard a small boat that was lowered from the *Santa Anita* down to the river. As the vessel slipped away toward the dock, Anita looked anxiously at the water. She knew what lurked there. Piranha were lured to the docks when fishermen threw out dead fish. Anita knew how vicious their bite was. Her brother Hansi had been bitten by one while dangling his feet off a dock, and she could still remember his cries as Arnold pulled him onto the deck and ripped the piranha off his foot.

Suddenly, just as she feared, the piranha swarmed, and the water boiled up as the greedy fish ravaged whatever prey they had found. The disturbance in the water caused the boat to rock and sway. For a moment, she froze in terror, but the skipper of the boat just laughed. Anita shuddered and reached for Don's hand. He smiled and put his arm around her.

The boat steadied as they pulled up next to the dock. The waters were calm there. Nevertheless, Anita was very careful as she moved about the boat, distrustful of every step. She anxiously took Don's offered hand as he easily lifted her to the dock's wooden floor.

A shout from the shore caught her attention. It was Rudi, her twin brother, waiting with a wagon to take them to the village.

"So, this is your monkey!" he laughed good-naturedly, extending his arm to shake Don's hand. Don returned the smile and the handshake. He already knew about the family joke and took no offense.

"And I am looking forward to getting to know my jungle family— my wife's family." They all laughed, and Anita beamed, sure that her new husband would fit right in.

"Well, let's get going. We've got a long way to go!" Rudi gestured to the wagon with two harnessed oxen. Anita groaned. She knew what lay ahead. The road to the village led through the pampas, and it was the muddy season. There would be hours of bone-jarring misery over the log road. Slender tree trunks, laid side by side, kept the road from sinking into the mud and ensured that the wagon's occupants would arrive with aching bones and no appetite.

Hours later, they made it to Tiefenbrunn, disheveled and exhausted. Anita worried about her homecoming. She had left home belligerently, and she didn't know how her family would treat her now. Would they remember her frustrated remarks about their way of life and resent her return? Would they accept her husband even though he was not a Mennonite?

To her surprise, there in the heat of the Paraguayan afternoon stood her whole family, smiling and welcoming her back. Humbled, Anita

received their hugs and kind words with a grateful heart. Even better, they cordially greeted her American husband with enthusiastic words of congratulations. Apparently, the elders had agreed that since he was from a Baptist family, a Mennonite pastor could officiate the wedding. Don, with his pleasant manner and big smile, acted quite at ease among a community of strangers. Her anxiety gone, Anita's eyes filled with tears as she listened to the plans her family had made for the wedding.

Being a Mennonite wedding, the event required days of preparation, especially the baking. It was a huge affair. Twelve villages were invited to the outdoor service, and the church choir planned to sing at the banquet. Each family would bring food to share, including an abundance of wonderful Mennonite desserts. The whole day would be filled with fellowship between friends who seldom saw each other.

This wedding was particularly momentous. It seemed everyone had heard of this feisty daughter-turned-city-girl. And, of course, everyone wanted to meet the American Marine who had captured her heart.

Of special interest were the movie projector and generator that Don brought from the embassy. He set the equipment up in a clearing, and there was standing room only as he played *Snow White and the Seven Dwarves* and *Sergeant York*. Even the natives could be seen peeking through the edges of the jungle to watch. Although movies were not an approved Mennonite activity, no one objected to Don's choice of films, and there was great enthusiasm.

No one was happier to see Anita than her little dog, Boquerón. His excitement was unbounded. With less enthusiasm, he accepted Don, but a neighbor's dog was less friendly. When Don tried to pet it, the dog bit him on the arm. Within a day, a nasty red streak of infection broke out on his skin. Fortunately, Anita's father, being a veterinarian, knew just what to do. With soap, water, and a poultice, the infection disappeared quickly.

Anita and Boquerón in Tiefenbrunn

The next week was spent taking various excursions in the jungle on horseback. Don had never ridden a horse before but quickly adapted. He particularly enjoyed hunting with his military sidearm and learned to use a machete from Anita's brothers. As Anita had hoped, her new husband earned the respect

Don and Alice in Tiefenbrunn

of her family and was well-liked by her father and brothers.

Soon, they were back on the boat headed downriver for Asunción. It was difficult to say goodbye to her family. She and Don would be leaving for America in a few months, and she recognized that it could be years before she would see her family again—if ever. During the trip, a quiet moment on the deck gave her time to reflect on all that she had experienced in her short life.

She thought of the last words her brother said before she left: "Anita, God protected us through the war. There is a reason you are still alive." Helmut was very gentle, taking her hand and looking into her eyes. "You owe Him your gratitude, at least. When you get to America, promise me you will go to church."

"Well, I won't go to a Mennonite church," she said haughtily and shrugged. "I'll find a Baptist church."

Alone on the deck, her eyes filled with tears as she recalled the conversation. She knew her brother was right. There were so many times that she and her family had miraculously been rescued. Yet, here she was, turning her back on God, her family, and the very community that had just given her a beautiful wedding.

Back in Asunción, Anita and Don rented a small, gated house near the embassy. They contracted a maid, Elsa, who did the cleaning, shopping, and cooking, and they acquired a dachshund named Dede. Anita was relieved to give all her duties to Elsa because she hated housework and had never bothered to learn how to cook. Besides, embassy work involved a very busy social schedule. Almost every night the couple attended social clubs for dancing and drinks. Life was certainly more exciting than anything Anita had known before, and thoughts of gratitude to a God she did not understand drifted further from her mind.

At Sugarloaf Mountain in Rio de Janeiro

Six months later, Don's transfer was settled, and the couple began their journey. Papers in hand, they traveled first to Buenos Aires, then to Brazil, then by plane to America, and finally by train to Brooklyn, New York. They stayed for a week in Brooklyn with Don's family.

Chapter 37
Shattered Self-Confidence

It was one of those beautiful autumn days in New York where the air seemed so clear it sparkled. Today, Anita and Don were going to visit Times Square, the busiest and most exciting place to see in the city. Anita looked around, thrilled at the hustle and bustle of her surroundings.

A sense of triumph ran through her, putting a click in her step. Anita grinned. She had done it. She had met and married an American. Now, here she was, in America, just like she had planned. She had set goals and achieved them. Feeling very confident, Anita strode out to the street where Don was hailing a taxi. Life was turning out just as she wanted, and it felt like nothing could stop her.

The trip across the Brooklyn Bridge and through Manhattan was exhilarating. There were so many gigantic buildings and so many people. It was like nothing she'd ever seen. Anita's mind wandered back to her little village in Ukraine and then to the refugee camps and the jungles of Paraguay. She smiled to herself as she remembered the hunger of wartime and the miserable heat of the jungle. That was not for her. This is what she wanted—life in the big city!

As the couple stepped out of the

Don and Anita in New York

taxi, Anita took in the busy scene and grinned. Everywhere she looked, there were people—walking in crowds, stopping to take photos, shopping, and brushing past one another without a glance. Shielding her eyes from the sun, she gazed up at the skyline. The tops of the buildings were not even visible. Back on the streets, the traffic was unbelievable. The cars inched back and forth, driving bumper to bumper and blaring their horns when someone moved too slowly. In comparison to the chattering hum of the jungle, the sounds of the city were deafening, yet Anita felt invigorated. Slowly, the couple made their way up the street through the masses.

The drone of an airplane in the distance caught Anita's attention, but she could not locate it because of the tall buildings. The noise from the plane grew louder.

Suddenly, the plane was overhead. Anita froze. Memories flooded over her while instinct told her to run for shelter. In her mind, the building above her collapsed as a bomb burst in the upper floors. Imagined flames leaped and swirled, reaching for her menacingly. The next building tumbled as its walls caught fire. Bombs exploded all around. The wall beside her crumbled. Ahead, the buildings began to fall into the street.

Fear overwhelmed her thoughts. There was nowhere to hide. Any moment now, she would be crushed beneath the rubble. Her breath came in short gasps as panic took over. Darkness closed around her, and she sank to the sidewalk.

"God, help me," she gasped. "I don't want to die!" A sense of dread hung heavily on her heart. She was going to die here, and there was nothing she could do about it. Sobbing, she sank against a wall.

"Anita, what's wrong?" Don reached her side, pushing aside strangers who had stopped to stare at her. Breathless, Anita could not answer as he firmly lifted her back to her feet. Don brought his wife inside a nearby lobby and found her a place to sit.

Gradually, with Don holding her hand, Anita's fear subsided, and her breathing returned to normal. She wanted to explain, but she couldn't form the words to describe what she had just seen. The trip back to Brooklyn was spent in complete silence.

Chapter 38
Reluctant Compliance

A week later, Don and Anita boarded a train bound for the West Coast. Don had been transferred to the Marine base at Camp Pendleton, California. So, the couple left the big city and headed to the quiet coastal town of Oceanside, situated halfway between Los Angeles and San Diego.

During the long hours of travel, Anita had some time to think about her situation. She always considered herself to be self-reliant and strong, but now, strangely, she no longer felt in control of her life. The recent experience in Times Square had shaken her soul.

"You can't run from God." Helmut's words played over and over in her mind.

Anita began to realize that running could be exactly what she was trying to do. She wanted her way, not the way of her parents or her community, and not God's way.

Somewhere between New York and California, Anita determined that since God apparently existed and had protected her and her family, she needed to pay more attention. She would look for a church—but on her terms.

Once in Oceanside, Don found a small vacation cottage on the beach. Since it was late October, the cottage was vacant. Anita stepped out from the house right onto the sand, enjoying long walks on the beach while Don was at the Marine base.

One afternoon not long after the couple moved in, some children came to the house dressed in costumes. They pounded on the door and yelled, "Trick or treat!"

Anita had no idea what they wanted and slammed the door shut. They knocked again and chanted, "Trick or treat," obviously expecting something. Anita opened the door again and asked what they wanted.

"Candy!" they yelled in unison.

"I have no candy," she said, taking a step back.

One child peeped past her to the table and said, "How about your apples? We can take those."

Relieved and a little shaken, Anita handed the apples to the children and away they went. When Don returned home from the base, he got a big laugh out of his wife's cultural introduction to Halloween. There would be several of these lessons over the next few months, but one of the most important happened the next Sunday.

The day before, Anita had taken a walk to town in search of a church, keeping her promise to her brother—and, as she supposed, to God. Reaching a big intersection, she saw a church on each corner. How was she supposed to choose? Remembering that Don had said his parents went to a Baptist church, she hoped one of them would be from that denomination. Sure enough, First Baptist Church of Oceanside was among the options. She entered and found a pamphlet that listed the morning service time. That night, she informed Don they would go to church the next day. He was surprised and not particularly interested, but he agreed.

The next day, the couple took a short walk from home to the church. The service began with typical songs sung from a hymnal. Shocked, Anita recognized the first tune. It was "What a Friend We Have in Jesus." Years ago, she had sung the same tune in Hitler Youth. She studied the words in the hymnal to see if they were the same. She didn't think that Americans would sing to Hitler.

The pastor preached a long message. Anita was not impressed. However, when they sang another song at the end, Don quietly raised his hand. To her surprise, a man sitting behind them tapped him on the shoulder, and together they walked to the front and disappeared into another room. Anita did not know why he would leave her there alone.

All the church members filed out, and Anita was left by herself.

She walked out to the sidewalk. She began to wonder if the church had taken her husband away just like the government had taken so many of her loved ones in Russia. Could that happen in America? Would he come back? Anxious and angry, she stood there alone, considering what to do.

But before long, Don returned—and he was grinning. Anita fumed at his delay, but there was no time to fuss because Don brought someone to introduce to her. His name was Joe Pelagi, and he invited the Barbers to have lunch with his family. Joe and his wife, Virginia, had five young children, and the four adults crammed into their car.

***

That Sunday at First Baptist Church of Oceanside, Anita had no idea that the Spirit of God had moved and convicted her husband or that his tough Marine heart had responded in repentance. Don knew very little of the Bible or the love of God despite growing up with a Baptist family. He was hungry for the truth, and, as is so often the case, God sent a young pastor in Vista to meet that need. The Pelagis felt a God-given responsibility to teach Don, a new believer, about God's Word. Joe met with Don almost every day in Oceanside to study the Bible. Consequently, Don grew in knowledge and faith—and Anita noticed. Little did she know that it would be the beginning of a new adventure for them both.

***

As summertime approached, Don and Anita needed a new place to live because the beach house would be rented out to vacationers. Fortunately, the Pelagis offered to share their farmhouse in Vista, a small town nearby. Surrounded by a loving and active Christian family, Anita began awakening to the Holy Spirit's whispers of her own resistance.

Anita had learned about God's love from her family in Paraguay. No longer under the bondage of Stalin's atheistic message and Hitler's control, her parents had taught her the gospel. She had memorized the Mennonite catechism and was aware that Jesus, God's Son, died for the sins of the world, but they were just words to her. Anita had not truly met the Savior.

Meanwhile, Mrs. Pelagi began holding a Good News Club for the children of her area. They met at her home, sang, played games, and listened to a story from the Bible. She enlisted Anita's help to assist with crowd control and crafts. In time, she went with Mrs. Pelagi to a child evangelism training class. A very gentle and gracious lady named Bernice Howard was the instructor. Mrs. Howard took special interest in Anita and came to Vista each week to meet with her, reading and explaining the Bible stories. Anita's proud heart began to melt under the kind and genuine love that Mrs. Howard demonstrated. It wasn't long before the Holy Spirit's conviction became impossible to ignore.

Chapter 39
The Day of Salvation

"Anita, you have been so helpful with our Good News Club. Maybe you would like to teach the Bible lesson next week," Mrs. Howard said to Anita as they gathered the paper scraps and sticky glue bottles left over from the children's craft project.

Hesitantly, Anita looked up and nodded. "Sure. I'll give it a try, but you need to help me."

Mrs. Howard picked through her pile of flannelgraph figures and Bible storybooks, handing Anita the materials for the next lesson.

"You can study this for next week. If you have any questions, I'll try to clarify it for you."

Anita opened the booklet and saw the first picture to show the children. She froze. Suddenly, she was taken back to long ago when she and her brother sat on her grandmother's couch in the Ukranian village.

Before her lay the scene of writhing snakes and screaming people, reaching out to a man holding a snake impaled on a stake. It was the very same picture Anita had seen in the unfamiliar Bible that she and Rudi discovered when they were eleven. It had captivated her then, and it held her spellbound now. This was no mere coincidence.

"Anita, what's wrong?" asked Mrs. Howard, putting her hand on Anita's shoulder.

"I know this picture. I saw it years ago." Anita's grip tightened on the booklet.

"Do you know what it means?" Her words were gentle.

Anita let out a long breath. She met Mrs. Howard's eyes and shook her head. She muttered, "Stay away from snakes."

"Yes, but more than that, it is about sin. God preserved the Israelites with many incredible miracles, yet they doubted God and kept asking God to prove Himself—and He did, but it was never enough for them. Their hearts were disloyal, and they rebelled against God. He sent fiery serpents to punish them for their sin. Many of them died, but God through Moses told the people that if they just looked up at the serpent on the stick, they would be healed."

Mrs. Howard continued, "The serpents came as a judgment for sin, but God provided a way to be healed from their poison. That serpent on the stick is a symbol, a message God gave about Christ who came to provide a way of deliverance from our sin. We are all broken, captive to the devil's schemes, but Christ offers us salvation. When we believe in Him, we will be saved from the judgment we deserve for our own disloyal hearts."

She pointed to the text. "Here, read these verses."

And as Moses lifted up the serpent in the wilderness, even so must the Son of man be lifted up: that whosoever believeth in him should not perish, but have eternal life. (John 3:14-15)

"That's Jesus, isn't it? The Son of man," Anita looked up.

"Yes," replied Mrs. Howard. "He was 'lifted up' on the cross to die, sentenced to death in judgment for our sins. And when we believe in Him, we will be saved from the wrath of God. If you just look up to Him in faith, knowing that He paid the price for our rebellion, He promises that we will have eternal life. This is the Good News that we share with the children."

"Oh, and the next verse is the one they memorized," Anita exclaimed as she looked down at the lesson again.

For God so loved the world, that he gave his only begotten Son, that whosoever believeth in him should not perish, but have everlasting life. (John 3:16)

"Yes, this verse is so much more vivid when you see it in context, isn't it?" Mrs. Howard said. "The image of the dead snake impaled on a pole is a powerful picture of how ugly our sin is to God. He sees our sin down to the depths of our hearts. Like the fiery serpent, Jesus died so we could be healed. There is a difference, though—that snake stayed dead, but Jesus came back to life. When we recognize the terrible price that Jesus paid to save us, it should compel us to trust Him. Just think, Jesus did it because He loves me and He loves you!"

Sensing that Anita was thinking this through, Mrs. Howard turned away, leaving the Holy Spirit to finish His work in her heart.

"See you tomorrow. Call me if you have questions." And she picked up her things and headed out.

The words of the Bible burned in Anita's heart all that day and into the evening. Snakes of all kinds crawled across her thoughts as she struggled with the meaning that pressed upon her. She knew she had a rebellious heart. She had rejected her family's faith and authority. Often she rebelled against the authority of God Himself. Just as she had been taught in school, she had at times even decided that God did not exist. She had excused her sin for so long, thinking of herself as strong and self-reliant—and never thinking of herself as evil. She wasn't that bad. Did she really need to repent? Wasn't she good enough for a merciful God to accept? Since coming to America, she'd tried to live like a Christian. It hadn't been easy. Why wasn't that enough for Him?

Somehow, in her mind she heard another verse the children had memorized and repeated it over and over again.

For all have sinned, and come short of the glory of God. (Romans 3:23)

In the late evening, in the unseen place of her heart, the Holy Spirit won the battle against the devil and his lies. Anita fell to her knees and confessed that she was a rebellious and guilty woman who had never lived up to Jesus' standard. Her only hope lay in looking up to that form on the cross, the perfect Son of God who gave His life to save hers, the One who shed His blood for her. In that moment, she accepted His free gift and placed her trust in Jesus.

She stood up a new creation, forgiven and cleansed. Anita had found freedom in Christ.

As Anita began to walk toward the phone to call Don and tell him all that had happened, she sensed the change in herself. The modern world with its conveniences and ease of life had lost its luster. All the lies she had been fed as a child—with all that Stalin and Hitler said about her purpose—had faded. None of it measured up to the truth she held in her heart. Eternal glory was in her sights now, greater than any adventure she'd ever sought. This goal was so far beyond her that she felt helpless to attain it, and yet God, in His infinite kindness, had promised it to her.

In the years to come, Anita would battle scars, fears, and pain of the past. She would fight her pride and self-reliance, her selfishness and hardness of heart, but she would never lose the deep sense of joy she had in knowing her Savior, Jesus Christ.

Epilogue

The seed of truth that had been sown long ago in Anita's heart began to grow. It received water from faithful Christians as the light of the Holy Spirit emerged. God faithfully preserved Anita through difficult and deadly situations, leading her to a place of trust in His atonement for her sin. In the same way He protected the Israelites in the desert, God demonstrated His deep love for Anita by intervening in her life again and again. By all odds, she should not have survived. Yet, by the grace of God, she did.

From that point on, Anita never forgot the debt she owed to her Savior. She became a dynamic and unstoppable witness to God's love and raised four children of her own. Her firstborn, Donald, is my husband, and I can attest that he is a godly testimony of his parents' determination to raise children for the Lord's service. He sometimes reveals that her enthusiasm for the discipline she learned under Stalin and Hitler marked the pattern of his upbringing. Yet, that severity was channeled toward the need to "walk worthy of the vocation wherewith ye are called," as taught in Ephesians 4:1.

After gaining American citizenship, Anita became a foster mom. Over the next thirty or so years, she helped raise more than 400 children. The training of Hitler Youth taught girls that they were to be mothers of a new Aryan race and raise children to serve the German state. As a foster mother, Anita was resolved to raise children to serve their Creator. Without exception, she prayed over all of them and committed each child to the Lord's service. She did the same with the parents who adopted them.

Even in her declining years, Anita found ways to work with children. She taught Bible stories in the Good News Club and shared the gospel with each child who made her acquaintance. Her passion for evangelism never waned. Every conversation turned to the love of Jesus and God's grace. Her faithful witness was an inspiration to all who knew her.

From the steppes of Ukraine to the golden state of California, God protected Anita through hunger, privation, and the dangers of war and sea. The poison of atheistic propaganda, the lure of worldly desires, and a rebellious heart had almost taken her captive, but the love of God prevailed, and Anita was preserved until the day that she surrendered her heart to Him. Today, she resides in heaven, safe for eternity.

Anita Friesen Barber

September 7, 1930–February 7, 2020

Bibliography

Dyck, Cornelius J., ed. 1993. *An Introduction to Mennonite History: A Popular History of the Anabaptist and the Mennonites*, 3rd ed. Scottdale, PA: Herald Press.

Dyck, Peter and Elfrieda. 1991. *Up From the Rubble: The Epic Rescue of Thousands of War-Ravaged Mennonite Refugees*. Scottdale, PA: Herald Press.

Linde, Hertha. 1997. *So Waren Wir. Bildband zur Geschichte des Bund Deutscher Mädel*. München: Brienna Verlag.

Quiring, Walter and Helen Bartel. 1974. *In the Fullness of Time: 150 Years of Mennonite Sojourn in Russia*, 3rd ed. Kitchener, Ontario: A. Klassen.

Schroeder, William and Helmut T. Heubert. 1996. *Mennonite Historical Atlas*, 2nd ed. Winnipeg, Canada: Springfield Publishers.

Image Credits

The maps on pages 17-19 and 109-110 are from William Schroeder and Helmut T. Huebert, 1996, *Mennonite Historical Atlas*, 2nd ed., Winnipeg, Canada: Springfield Publishers, and are used courtesy of the Centre for Mennonite Brethren Studies.

The pictures on pages 37b, 39, 48, 50-51, and 59 are from Walter Quiring and Helen Bartel, 1974, *In the Fullness of Time: 150 Years of Mennonite Sojourn in Russia*, 3rd ed., Kitchener, Ontario: A. Klassen.

About the Author

Rebecca Morris Barber was raised in the beautiful town of Blacksburg, Virginia. She and her husband, Don, began their ministry at a Bible camp, he as director, she as song leader and horseback riding instructor. Her ministry expanded to coaching various sports while homeschooling their three children. Eventually, her interest in nature and science led her to become certified as an herbalist to explore the natural remedies that God has provided for His creation. Today she and Don are involved in the ministry of the Institute for Creation Research. She is also the author of *Henry M. Morris: Father of Modern Creationism.*

About the
Institute for Creation Research

At the Institute for Creation Research, we want you to know God's Word can be trusted with everything it speaks about—from how and why we were made, to how the universe was formed, to how we can know Jesus Christ and receive all He has planned for us.

That's why ICR scientists have spent more than 50 years researching scientific evidence that refutes evolutionary philosophy and confirms the Bible's account of a recent and special creation. We regularly receive testimonies from around the world about how ICR's cutting-edge work has impacted thousands of people with Christ's creation truth.

How Can ICR Help You?

You'll find faith-building science articles in *Acts & Facts*, our bimonthly science news magazine, and spiritual insight and encouragement from *Days of Praise*, our quarterly devotional booklet. Sign up for FREE at **ICR.org/subscriptions**.

Our radio programs, podcasts, online videos, and wide range of social media offerings will keep you up to date on the latest creation news and announcements. Get connected at **ICR.org**.

We offer creation science books, DVDs, and other resources for every age and stage at **ICR.org/store**.

Learn how you can attend or host a biblical creation event at **ICR.org/events**.

Discover how science confirms the Bible at our Dallas museum, the ICR Discovery Center. Plan your visit at **ICRdiscoverycenter.org**.

ICR
INSTITUTE FOR CREATION RESEARCH

P. O. Box 59029
Dallas, TX 75229
800.337.0375
ICR.org